100 Poems from the Chinese:

From the *Shijing* to Mao Zedong

Translated by Earl Trotter

Peach Blossom Press

Peach Blossom Press
Chatham, ON

Cover illustration: Lin Bu with Plum Blossoms and Crane
Author's collection.

Trotter, Earl
100 Poems from the Chinese: From the *Shijing* to Mao Zedong
Includes bibliographical references.
ISBN: 978-1-7780422-4-9

1. Chinese Poetry—Translation. 2. Chinese poetry—Anthology

For My Granddaughter,

Huang Qiuqing

黄秋晴

Table of Contents

Introduction

Chinese poetry has a history of about three thousand years. Although features have varied widely over that time, certain standard elements predominate.

The Character and Line

The elemental unit is the character. Usually one character has one sound and a specific meaning. Occasionally, two characters are grouped together to determine the meaning, but this was less common in classical Chinese. There is also a caesura or pause within a line which is determined by form or line length.

The line length can vary but in the earliest period, a four-character line was common. Over time the five-character line came to predominate with a caesura after the second character. In the Tang dynasty (618-907), seven-character lines also became common, with the caesura after the fourth character. Finally, certain forms (see below) have a variable line length.

Couplets and Stanzas

Classical Chinese verse usually has a couplet structure. The two lines may be related by meaning, but also by rhyme, and later in the Tang, by tones. Note that rhyme is quite common, but due to the shifting of sounds over the centuries, not all rhyme is aurally detectable in modern Chinese although documented rhyme words aid in determining what may have rhymed. The rhyme scheme may also extend beyond the couplet. Building on the couplet structure, many poems are four-line quatrains or eight-line octets. This turned out to be the norm although certain forms were longer (sometimes very long). These are usually forms following a specific song or ballad prototype.

There are various rules on the use of words which we will not go into here, other than say, pronouns and many grammatical particles are usually not employed, leading to a certain ambiguity of meaning. Other rules are specific to given eras or forms.

Poetic Forms

We will discuss four poetic forms or genres: *shi*, *fu*, *yuefu*, and *ci*.

Shi **(詩)**

This is the term used for poetry in general. But in a more narrow sense, it refers to poems with a fixed-length line, usually of four, five, or seven characters. They have a couplet structure and use rhyme, parallelism and later, various tonal structures, to unite the piece. Moving into the Tang dynasty, a four- or eight-line length prevailed and new rules were introduced, especially relating to tones, resulting in regulated verse. The basic *shi* structure originated in the *Shijing* or *Book of Songs* (11th cent. BCE – 7th cent. BCE).

Fu **(賦)**

Fu, often translated "rhapsody", is not strictly speaking poetry and is unlike any Western genre. However there is rhyme and the rhymed lines are of equal length, so it is at least, a semi-poetic form. It arose during the Han dynasty (206 BCE – AD 220). It is usually viewed as having developed from the *Chu Ci* or *Verses of Chu* (3rd cent. BCE). A locale, thing, thoughts and feelings, are explored extensively in the exposition. They are usually long as they are meant to be exhaustive and the non-rhymed sections have various line lengths. The vocabulary, given the length and detailed exposition, is usually quite extensive. The form started to decline in the Song dynasty (960–1279).

Yuefu (樂府)

Yuefu are Chinese poems composed in a folk song style, specifically, those based on materials gathered by the Music Bureau during the Han dynasty. During the Han and Six Dynasties (220-589), poets wrote poems based on this collection and produced what is known as literary *yuefu*. The lines can be of uneven length. In the Tang, new *yuefu* developed, often using the five- or seven-character line, common to the era. The subject matter can be almost anything.

Ci (詞)

Ci is a lyrical form using poetic meters from a base set of patterns with a given rhythm, tone, and variable line-length. The rhythmic and tonal pattern of the *ci* are based upon musical song tunes. The were about 800 set patterns, each with a particular title. Any poem using a named pattern would have that title regardless of subject matter and a number of poems could share the same title. *Ci* usually express personal feelings but Su Shi (1037–1101) transformed the genre by tackling other subject matter. This led to an explosion of *ci* poems in the Song dynasty. It popularity waned after that although there was a late Ming dynasty (1368–1644) revival.

A Brief Sketch of the History of Chinese Poetry

The Book of Songs (*Shijing*) is the fountainhead of Chinese poetry. Not only the poems therein but the later Mao Commentary had an enormous influence. Although mostly folk songs, once the collection was admitted to the Confucian canon, allegorical political interpretations were applied to many pieces. The poetry influenced succeeding verse indirectly, if not directly.

The next important collection was the *Chu Ci*, primarily by Quan Yu (c. 340 BCE – 278 BCE). Besides providing images and quotes for later poetry it set the foundation for the development of the *fu*. Finally, in the Han dynasty, the Nineteen Ancient Songs also had an impact on later poetry and helped set the standard for the five-character line.

In the Han dynasty, the *Book of Songs* had a great influence. As well, the fu form developed based on the impetus given by the *Chu Ci*. As previously mentioned, the Music Bureau's collection of folk songs, led to the development of literary *yuefu*.

The Six Dynasties was the next great flourishing of poetic development. Besides a move to the five-character line, we have the establishment of Fields and Gardens poetry (田园诗) by Tao Yuanming and *Shanshui* or Landscape poetry (山水詩) by Xie Lingyun. Tao Yuanming was especially a great influence in the Tang Dynasty and thereafter.

The Tang dynasty was the pinnacle of Classical Chinese poetry, headed by the likes of Wang Wei (701–759), Li Bai (701–762) and Du Fu (712–770). During the Tang, the importance of tones was realized and applied to prosody and left a mark on all subsequent poetry. Most of the current anthology is the work of Tang poets.

The Song dynasty recognized the greatness of the Tang poets but developed a more sophisticated approach to verse which was basically a move from the feelings to the intellect and a greater interest in politics, both in their own poems and in the interpretation of past works. The *ci* form also gained ascendancy here. The surviving output of Song poets greatly exceeds that of the Tang. The most important poet here is Su Shi.

In the Yuan dynasty, the opera gained prominence and the *qu* (曲), basically operatic arias, became dominant. In the Ming (1368–1644) and Qing (1636–1912) the novel came to the fore. However, there are still interesting poets such as Yuan Mei (1716–1798) and perhaps there is more hidden ore here. Classical Chinese poetry came to an end with the writing of Hu Shi (1891–1962) but some continued to write in the old manner such as Mao Zedong (1892–1976).

The five most important poets in the history of Chinese poetry are Tao Yuanming (also known as Tao Qian), Wang Wei, Li Bai, Du Fu, and Su Shi (also known as Su Dongpo). One could come up with alternative lists but each would likely include at least three of these. Of course there are many other excellent poets, any of whom, may appeal to one's personal taste.

About The Translation

I have given priority to meaning. Although across such a span of time and cultures, one cannot be expected to catch every nuance, still an approximation to the original is possible. So, from a twenty-first century's reader's perspective, I try and capture and present the intended meaning as much as possible.

As to structure I have tried to replicate to some degree the original structure. What this means in practice, is that the lines are left intact, that the couplet remains as a unit for the five-character verse and that word order is preserved. The couplet, which is usually two distinct clauses, is most frequently divided by a semicolon after the first line. Sometimes the lines are end stopped, especially where a question or exclamation is involved. Sometime the lines run on if the sense demands it. In the odd case, four lines may make a unit. As for seven-character lines, I have split and indented the last part of the line and end-stopped each line. Having the full fourteen-character couplet as one sentence seemed to be stretching it. For word order, as these poems are so remote in time and culture, inversions do not seem a problem. If too awkward, I have changed the order around. Leaving the lines intact has occasionally resulted in an unusually long or short line, but these are rare and I have left it as is.

As for sound, I have for the most part ignored rhyme, alliteration and so on. It would be very difficult to introduce these features without compromising the meaning. As well, the pronunciation in modern Chinese is different, so to a native Chinese reader the sound of the poem no longer matches the original, although some parallels would be present.

The Chinese text is in traditional characters and in the translation, names and places are rendered in pinyin. About the only term I haven't translated is "*li*" as it often (though not always) is used in symbolic expressions of great distance. The *li* is about one third of a mile. Also "the ten thousand things" is sometimes translated as such and sometimes as "myriad things." Its basic meaning is "everything" although there might be specific nuances ("nature", "heaven and earth"…).

Although there is further commentary at the beginning of each chapter and also notes on the individual poets, the reader seeking more in-depth information should refer to the books listed in the Selected Bibliography. *The Indiana Companion to Chinese Literature* was helpful in getting information on most of the lesser known poets. Only the five poets alluded to above as being the most important have individual entries in the bibliography. The remaining references cover collections, eras, genres, or Chinese poetry in general. This anthology is, of course, highly selective. Those looking for a broader range should refer to Barnstone's *The Anchor Anthology of Chinese Poetry* and Liu and Lo's *Sunflower Splendor* (see Selected Bibliography).

The Beginnings

Zhou Dynasty (1122 BCE–256 BCE)

Chinese recorded history begins with the Zhou Dynasty. It was during this period that the *Shijing* or *Book of Songs* was written down. We will cover it further in the section with selections from this work but to repeat what was said in the Introduction, it is the wellspring of the future poetry to come. In the latter part of the Zhou, the Eastern Zhou (770 BCE–256 BCE), the great thinkers appeared: Confucius, Mengzi, Laozi and Zhuangzi. In the *Laozi* (it is the name attributed to the man and the work), there is some verse of note. Following them, the Hundred Schools of Thought arose including Confucianism, Legalism, Daoism, Mohism, the School of Yin-yang, and the School of Names, to name the most important.

During the waning years of the Zhou, Qu Yuan appeared and his writing along with some others, were collected in the *Chu Ci* or *Verses of Chu*. Again, we will deal with this in the selection section, but note here once more, that the *fu* developed from his work. The Zhou was succeeded in 256 BCE by the short-lived Qin dynasty which was of lesser importance in the literary field.

Han Dynasty (202 BCE–220 CE)

The Han dynasty saw the growth of agriculture and a robust economy. Also, most aspects of culture and government took form which would persist until modern times. Confucianism became the state religion and the civil service or imperial examination system, based on the Confucian classics, was instituted. The dynasty began with the Western Han centered in Chang'an, and the last half of the dynasty, the Eastern Han, had its capital in Luoyang.

The *Verses of Chu* was assembled in this period. As well, the *fu* took form and were popular. The Music Bureau was established and *yuefu*, or folk songs, were gathered or written. New poems written under the influence of this collection, known as literary *yuefu* became widespread. The *Nineteen Ancient Poems*, to be discussed in the appropriate section, were written during the Han. In addition to being esteemed as poetry, their five-character line eventually led to the dominance of that form.

The Six Dynasties (220–589)

The Han finally ended in 220 and was followed by the chaotic Three Kingdoms (220–280). but the establishment of the Jin dynasty (220–420), inaugurated the Six Dynasties period. Confucianism declined somewhat, official Daoism flourished and Buddhism was introduced from India, becoming more important as time went by.

The five-character line continued to gain ascendancy. Meanwhile, the seven-character line began to become popular after the work of Bao Chao (414–466) who innovated with a ABCB rhyme scheme. As well, many *yuefu* and *fu* continued to be written. One of the first important poets was Cao Zhi (192–232). He was followed by the Sages of the Bamboo Grove. The most notable poets of this group were Ruan Ji (210–263) and Xi Kang (223–262), also known as Ji Kang. The next notable figure is Tao Yuanming (365–427), who was later seen as the father of Fields and Gardens poetry (田园诗). He rose to prominence as a poetic influence during the Tang dynasty. Then came the founder of Shanshui or Landscape poetry (山水詩), Xie Lingyun (385–433). While Tao's poetry tended to simplicity, Xie's was rather complex.

Later on "palace-style" poetry came to predominate with elaborate diction and flowery images. Many of them were collected in *New Songs from a Jade Terrace*. The rise of Tang dynasty poetry is partly a reaction against this and a return to Tao Yuanming's style. Although there were other fine poets, the most important have been mentioned above. The short-lived Sui dynasty (581–618) produced no poets of note.

The *Shijing* or *Books of Songs* (1100 BCE – 700 BCE)

The *Book of Songs* is the earliest collection of Chinese verse. The poems were likely written between the dates given above and gathered together shortly thereafter. They provided the matter and manner for subsequent poetry. Confucius refers to the *Book of Songs* and it became one of the Confucian classics, with the dubious assertion that Confucius himself was the compiler. The collection is a mixture of folk songs along with court and sacrificial pieces. Especially with the former one gets a glimpse at life at that time.

There are 305 pieces, most of which use the four-character line, with a caesura in the middle. The lines are in couplets. Parallelism and repetition of the first character in a line are sometimes seen. About half of the pieces are of the folk variety but they seem to been through the hands of the literati as they are formally structured. They were seen as moral or political allegories by Confucians in order to elevate the often basic, down-to-earth subject matter. But the folk-based poems or songs are best seen as primal expressions of the human heart. The four-character line prevailed for hundreds of years before giving way to the five-character line, not to mention, seven-character, as these allowed for a more extensive expression in each line.

Gathering Water Clover

She gathers water clover
on the banks of southern mountain streams.
And gathers water plants
in those flowing streams.

She puts them in containers,
secure in square and round bamboo baskets.
Later, she boils them
in cauldrons and pans.

She offers libations
beneath the window of the ancestral shrine.
Who is this medium of the spirits?
A pious girl, just coming of age.

Shijing or *Book of Songs* #15 (1100 BCE – 700 BCE)

采蘋

于以采蘋
南澗之濱
于以采藻
于彼行潦

于以盛之
維筐及筥
于以湘之
維錡及釜

于以奠之

宗室牖下
誰其尸之
有齊季女

詩經 其十五

The Quiet Girl

The quiet girl is beautiful;
she waits for me by the city walls.
I love her but do not see her –
I scratch my head, walking back and forth.

The quiet girl is lovely;
she gave me a red flute,
a red flute that glistens,
showing its joy at the girl's beauty.

Returning from the pasture, she gave me a tender shoot,
truly beautiful and unique –
it is not just its beauty,
but that the beautiful woman gave it.

Shijing or *Book of Songs* #43 (1100 BCE – 700 BCE)

靜女

靜女其姝
俟我於城隅
愛而不見
搔首踟躕

靜女其孌
貽我彤管
彤管有煒
說懌女美

自牧歸荑

洵美且異
匪女之為美
美人之貽

詩經 其四十三

Chu Ci or *Verses of Chu (3rd cent.* BCE? – ?)

The *Verses of Chu* is the second anthology of Chinese poetry after the *Book of Songs* and together they represent the bulk of early Chinese poetry. Many of the poems in the *Verses of Chu* are by Qu Yuan (c. 340 BCE–278 BCE), the first named Chinese poet. But before the book was finalized, other pieces, some about Qu Yuan, were added. The current version is based on Wang Yi's 2nd century work.

Qu Yuan was a member of the royal house of Chu but was admonished by King Huai (329 BCE– 299 BCE). He then wrote his most famous work (and the main work in the collection), *Li Sao* known as "Encountering Sorrow" or "The Lament" in English to show his loyalty. Later, after the king had died, his son banished Qu Yuan to the south and Qu Yuan drowned himself. Qu Yuan then became an exemplary Confucian figure and the Dragon Boat Festival is held every year in his honor. "The Lament" is a long elaborate poem which formed the basis of subsequent *fu*. Qu also made of use of parallelism in the couplets which influenced later Chinese poetry.

Other poems are in various formats and a variety of themes. There are the shamanistic "Nine Songs", the mythological "Heaven Questions" and "The Fisherman" in prose, from which we have translated the short song therein. In all there are seventeen sections, a number consisting of many individual pieces. The number nine appears in many of the section titles. Although the *Chu Ci* had a great influence in Chinese poetics, it doesn't reach the impact that the *Book of Songs* had.

The Fisherman's Song

Ah, when the Canglang's waters are clear,
there I can wash the tassels of my cap[1];
but when the Canglang's waters are muddy,
there I can wash my feet.

From 'The Fisherman' in the *Chu Ci* or *Verses of Chu*
(2nd cent. BCE?)

滄浪之水清兮。
可以濯吾纓。
滄浪之水濁兮。
可以濯吾足。

漁父 - 楚辭

1 An indicator of official status. Therefore, be an official when the state is just, otherwise retire from office.

Nineteen Ancient Poems (2nd cent.)

The *Nineteen Ancient Poems* were part of the *yuefu* tradition. They likely date from the 2nd century. They are anonymous pieces written in five-character meter and it from these poems that the five-character meter eventually became one of standard forms of versification in Chinese. The melancholic subject matter of love and the brevity of life prevalent in these pieces, became a common theme in later literature.

Nineteen Ancient Poems #1

On and on, and on and on –
from you, I must part.
We'll be ten thousand *li* apart,
each at opposite extremes of the sky.
The roads are long and blocked;
who knows where we'll meet again.
The Hu horse leans into the north wind;
the Yue[2] bird nests in southern branches.
Since the day I left you, I've gone so far;
since that day, my belt has grown loose.
Floating clouds cover the sun;
this traveller thinks not of turning back.
To think of you causes me to age –
years and months suddenly pass by.
Rejected, I'll speak of it no more –
I'll try hard and again, eat my fill.

(2nd cent.)

古詩十九首 - 其一

行行重行行，
與君生別離，
相去萬餘里，
各在天一涯。
道路阻且長，
會面安可知。
胡馬依北風，
越鳥巢南枝。

2 The Hu and Yue are peoples of the north and south respectively.

相去日已遠，
衣帶日已緩。
浮雲蔽白日，
遊子不顧反。
思君令人老，
歲月忽已晚，
棄捐勿復道，
努力加餐飯。

Ruan Ji (210–263)

Ruan Ji was born in what is now Henan province. His father was Ruan Yu, one of the Seven Scholars of Jian'an. He was a member of the Seven Sages of the Bamboo Grove, literati who retreated to a bamboo grove to talk, drink and practice their works. Ruan Ji was prime among them. He was a Daoist and much given to drink.

His poetry, tinged with Daoism, is expressive and shows both positive and negative emotions. Like the man, his work was often against Confucian values. The selection is the first piece of his five-character line sequence “Expressing My Feelings”.

Expressing My Feelings #1

The middle of the night and I can’t sleep!
I get up, sit, and strum sounds on my zither.
The bright moon reflects on my thin curtain;
a breeze blows against the front of my robe.
A solitary swan goose cries in a distant field,
while wheeling birds sing in the northern wood.
To and fro I pace – what will I meet up with?
Anxious thoughts wound my lonely heart.

Ruan Ji (210–263)

咏懷 – 其一

夜中不能寐，
起坐彈鳴琴。
薄帷鑒明月，
清風吹我襟。
孤鴻號外野，
翔鳥鳴北林。
徘徊將何見，
憂思獨傷心。

阮籍

Zhang Xie (?–307)

Zhang Xie was a Jin dynasty poet. Some say he was influenced by Wang Can (177-217). He is also reputed to be a link from Han dynasty *fu* to a later poetic style of verisimilitude (形似 *xingsi*), a term used to describe descriptive likeness.

Miscellaneous Poems #4

The red clouds of morning welcome the sun;
cinnabar vapors hang over Sunrise Vale[3].
Cloud after cloud forms
and a heavy rain falls.

A breeze devastates the flourishing grass,
as an icy frost makes tall trees rigid.
The dense leaves scatter day and night;
clusters of trees in the forest seem bundled together.

Long ago, I would sigh at time passing so slowly,
but in old age I mourn the swiftly fleeting years.
My twilight years are troubled by a hundred worries;
I will follow Ji Zhu[4] and become a diviner.

Zhang Xie (? -307)

雜詩四首

朝霞迎白日，
丹氣臨湯谷。
翳翳結繁雲，
森森散雨足。
輕風摧勁草，
凝霜竦高木。
密葉日夜疏，
叢林森如束。
疇昔嘆時遲，

3 A mythological valley where the sun bathes in a cinnabar pool before reascending.
4 A famous recluse-diviner of the kingdom of Chu

晚節悲年促。
歲暮懷百憂，
將從季主卜。

張協

Tao Yuanming (365-427)

Tao Yuanming was born in Chaisang (now in Jiangxi). At some time later in his life, he assumed the literary name, Tao Qian. His father died when he was young and he grew up in straightened circumstances. He seems to have left office about five times in the twelve-year timespan during which he held some position. For the last part of his life, he lived as a farmer and his most famous poems relate to this theme. Tao wrote in various forms: elegies, exchange poems, sacrificial songs, linked verse, love verse, admonitions, history. However he is best known for his Field and Garden (*tianyuan*) poetry as it was afterwards labelled. His style is plain and his feelings come across as sincere and this combination make these poems easy to appreciate across cultures and time.

As for Tao Yuanming's reception, in the latter part of his life and immediately after his death, he was seen primarily as a figure of reclusion (i.e. someone who refrains from office) who also wrote poetry. But the High Tang poets, also struggling with the demands of office versus inner development, esteemed Tao's poems and lifestyle and he was forever propelled into fame. The Song dynasty (960–1279) continued emulation of him, often with a more political slant.

Drinking Wine #5

I built my hut amidst the world of men
but there is no sound of cart or horse.
You ask how that can be –
the mind far from things is in itself quiet.
Gathering chrysanthemums by the eastern fence,
far off, I glance up at the Southern Mountains –
the mountain mists at dusk are beautiful
as birds together in flight return home.
In all this is the True Mind.
When I try to explain it, already I've forgotten the words.

Tao Yuanming (365-427)

飲酒二十首

其五

結廬在人境。
而無車馬喧。
問君何能爾。
心遠地自偏。
采菊東籬下。
悠然見南山。
山氣日夕佳。
飛鳥相與還。
此中有真意。
欲辨已忘言。

陶淵明

Drinking Wine #7

Autumn chrysanthemums have beautiful colors.
I pluck the petals, moistened with dew.
and float these in ‘forget about worries’ wine
to leave worldly affairs far behind.
Although I take a single cup alone,
when it’s empty I pour another from the flask.
The sun sets and the moving multitudes come to rest;
birds sing as they hasten home to the wood.
I whistle self-contentedly in the east pavilion –
bit by bit, I’m getting back my life.

Tao Yuanming (365-427)

飲酒二十首

其七

秋菊有佳色。
裛露掇其英。
泛此忘憂物。
遠我遺世情。
一觴雖獨進。
杯盡壺自傾。
日入群動息。
歸鳥趨林鳴。
嘯傲東軒下。
聊複得此生。

陶淵明

Returning to Live in the Country #4

For a long time I left wandering about hills and lakes,
roving with pleasure over grass, woods and fields.
So it was apt to take along my children and nephews
and push through a thicket to some desolate ruins.
We roamed between the mounds
then lingered by a dwelling from the past.
The well and hearth were all that remained
amidst rotten pieces of mulberry and bamboo.
I asked a wood gatherer happening by:
"Do you know what's happened to all these people?"
The wood gatherer replied to me:
"They're dead and gone, no one is left."
'In a single lifetime, court and markets change.'
This a true statement, not false.
A person's life is like illusory transformations
and at death returns to empty nothingness.

Tao Yuanming (365-427)

歸園田居

其四

久去山澤遊，
浪莽林野娛。
試攜子侄輩，
披榛步荒墟。
徘徊丘壟間，
依依昔人居；
井竈有遺處，
桑竹殘朽株。
借問採薪者：

此人皆焉如？
薪者向我言：
死殁無復餘。
一世異朝市，
此語真不虛。
人生似幻化，
終當歸空無。

Xie Lingyun (385-433)

Xie Lingyun was born in what is now Henan. He came from a wealthy family who were politically involved. Xie served in office but was banished. He later returned to his vast estate where he wrote a good deal of his nature poetry. He went back into office once more but had a rather abrasive character. After a few more ups and downs, he was executed in exile in Guangzhou,

Xie was the founder of *Shanshui* or Landscape poetry (山水詩), depicting the wilds of mountains and streams. Influenced by *fu* descriptive poetry he applied it to the natural landscape. His poetry is difficult but can be striking and did have an impact later generations. Xie studied Buddhism when young which may have influenced his work. One must remember when reading about his seemingly solo treks in the wild, that he had a large retinue helping him along with supplies and such. In any case, certainly a fine and important poet.

Following Jinzhu Stream, I Cross the Mountains and Trek along the River

At the cry of the gibbons, one indeed knows it's dawn;
but the valley is dim as the sun has yet to shine here.
Clouds are just forming beneath the cliffs
and the flowers still drip with dew.
Zigzagging anxiously along a winding stream,
I advance a long way up the steep mountain pass.
Having crossed the stream through strong rapids,
I tread the cliff plank-road that leads to distant hills.
The riverbank doubles back again and again:
I go with the flow and enjoy wandering about.
Masses of duckweed float on the depths;
wild rice and cattails shoot up from the clear shallows.
Tiptoe on a rock, I ladle out water from a cliffside spring
and scramble up to pick furled leaves in the forest.
I seem to see a mountain spirit
clad in a fig-leaf coat before my eyes.
Grasping asters, I try hard, in vain, to tie them;
I pluck hemp flowers but there is no one I can open up to.
It's the feeling heart that appreciates beauty;
this matter is obscure, in the end who can understand it?
Viewing all this I leave behind mundane concerns;
with one awakening, even gain is given up.

Xie Lingyun (385-433)

從斤竹澗越嶺溪行

猿鳴誠知曙，
谷幽光未顯。
岩下雲方合，

花上露猶泫。
逶迆傍隈隩，
迢遞陟陘峴。
過澗既厲急，
登棧亦陵緬。
川渚屢徑復，
乘流玩回轉。
蘋萍泛沉深，
菰蒲冒清淺。
企石挹飛泉，
攀林摘葉卷。
想見山阿人，
薜蘿若在眼。
握蘭勤徒結，
折麻心莫展。
情用賞為美，
事昧竟誰辨？
觀此遺物慮，
一悟得所遣。

謝靈運

Bo Daoyou (mid-5th century)

Little is known about Bo Daoyou. He must have had some association with Buddhist monks as it is recorded that he presented a poem to the monk Zhu Daoyi, who was delighted with it.

A Poem on Gathering Herbs in the Mountains

Peaks connected for thousands of miles
while tall trees girdle the steep plateau.
Clouds pass, covering the distant mountains;
the wind rises but is blocked by dense bush.

Secluded thatched cottages cannot be seen;
but by cock's crow one knows people live here.
I slowly walk along their paths
and everywhere see firewood left behind.

It dawns on me – a hundred generations like this
have lived here, under legendary rulers of old.

Bo Daoyou (mid-5th century)

陵峰采藥觸興為詩

連峰數千里，
修林帶平津。
雲過遠山翳，
風至梗荒榛。
茅茨隱不見，
雞鳴知有人。
間步踐其徑，
處處見遺薪
始知百代下，
故有上皇民。

帛道猷

Zhang Rong (443-497)

Zhang Rong was born in Jiangsi. He was secretary to the Prince of Xin'an. Captured once by bandits, he recited a poem, and impressed or astonished, they released him. His "Fu on the Sea" was popular at the time. The poem translated here seems to be his most famous.

A Poem of Parting (Miscellaneous Poem)

The white clouds have passed over the mountains;
a cool breeze lingers under the pines.
You wish to know the sorrow of one who must depart?
On a lonely tower, gaze at the bright moon.

Zhang Rong (444-497)

別詩

白雲山上盡
清風松下歇
欲識離人悲
孤台見明月

張融

Xie Tiao (464-499)

Xie Tiao was born in Yangxia, Henan. He came from the same prominent family as Xie Lingyun and in fact excelled at Landscape Poetry, like the latter, with detailed description of the beauties of nature. He often utilized the five-character line. Less than two hundred of his poems are extant. His work was admired by Li Bai, amongst others. He held high court positions but eventually antagonized a prince, was arrested, and died in prison at the age of thirty-five.

My Travelling Prince

The green grasses spread like silk threads;
on various trees, red blossoms bloom.
No matter if you don't come home –
if you did, the fragrant flowers would already be finished.

Xie Tiao (464-499)

王孫游

綠草蔓如絲。
雜樹紅英發。
無論君不歸。
君歸芳已歇。

謝朓

Tang Dynasty (618–907)

In the Tang dynasty, poetry reached its pinnacle. In turned away from the ornate "Palace Poetry" style and aimed at direct feeling or socio-political critiques. Often the latter had to be placed in the far past or was allegorical, in order to avoid censorship or even punishment for outspokenness. All facets of culture prospered and especially noteworthy is the establishment of Buddhism as a major religious and cultural force.

Tang History

Li Yuan became the first Tang emperor, Emperor Gaozu. The empire was gradually expanded. The Li family continued to reign but in 690 Wu Zetian, who started out as influential consort, maneuvered her way to become Empress and founded the Wu Zhou dynasty (690–705). The Li's were restored to power by a palace coup. The most significant ruler thereafter was Emperor Xuanzong who ruled 713-756. The most important poets flourished under his reign. After being an able ruler for the first part of his rule, he began to lose control. Later, his infatuation for Yang Guifei, led to his overthrow and her death. Amidst all this was the An Lushan Rebellion (755– 763) which threatened the empire but was eventually crushed. After this the Tang went into slow decline until its total collapse in 907.

Tang Poetics

The main innovation in Tang poetry was regulated verse or *lu shi*. Prior to the Tang, when scholars began translating Buddhist texts from India, they became aware of tones in their own language and identified four. The idea arose to employ the tones in systematic manner to poetry. It was in the Tang that this began to be applied most systematically. Speaking in general terms, the rule was to have tones at key positions in the line (especially 2 and 4), contrast within the couplet and match between the last couplet line, and first line of the next couplet. In this schema, there was the level tone and the other three were classed together as non-level. Such verse was called "regulated." There were also rules for word categories or parts of speech matching. As well the lines were either five- or seven-characters long and the poem length was four or eight lines. Poems not following this schema were "unregulated." Of course Tang poets continued to write in all the genres. They also revitalized the *yuefu* with new *yuefu* which extended this form in theme and style.

Tang Poetry and Poets

Tang poetry is usually divided into four periods: Early Tang, High Tang, Middle Tang and Late Tang. This is an arbitrary division and dates are approximative.

Early Tang (618–712)

At the very beginning, poets were still influenced by the "Palace-Style" poetry with its ornate and extravagant diction. There was a gradually change over the decades and with Wang Ji (585–644), who emulated Tao Yuanming, the move towards simplicity and frank expression gained hold. At the end of the period, the poetry of Chen Zi'ang (661–702) ushered in the new Tang style.

High Tang (713–765)

This is when the greatest poets came to the fore. Wang Wei (701–761) who wrote not only Buddhistic nature poetry but all kinds of formal and informal verse; Li Bai (701–762) with his

Daoist flight of vision and more; and Du Fu (712–770) with his Confucian social concern and who was perhaps the best poet.

Middle Tang (766–826)

Poets in this time frame built on the work of Du Fu and others. Frontier Poetry and Landscape Poetry were popular. One outstanding poet was Han Yu (768–824), who was also a great prose writer and urged a return, from Buddhist, to Confucian values. As well, Bai Juyi (772–846) aimed to write simple poetry that could be appreciated by all. His poetry proved popular and later he was lauded in Japan. Liu Zongyuan (773–819), although not so highly regarded as the other two was also a great prose writer and wrote some compelling poetry. Later in the Tang, Li He (790–816) foreshadowed the Late Tang with his imaginative expressionist pieces.

Late Tang (827–907)

There was a decline in the late Tang but some poets still shone. Du Mu (803–852) wrote both *shi* and *fu*. He wrote lyrical quatrains on love and history. Against a conservative basis he added a variety of wordplay which became popular in the Late Tang. Li Shangyin (813–858) on the other hand wrote complex and allusive poetry. Finally, at the very end of the dynasty, the last Tang Emperor, Li Yu (c. 937– 978), who was also a poet, wrote some fine *ci* which became the forerunner for the explosion of this genre in the following Song dynasty. However the end was in sight for both the Tang dynasty and the later style of poetry (outside the *ci*).

There were two important collections of Tang poetry made in the Qing dynasty. First, *The Complete Anthology of Tang Poetry* (*Quan Tangshi*) contains some fifty thousand poems by more than two thousand poets. The other collection which proved to be one of the most read anthologies was *300 Tang Poems* compiled by Sun Zhu. It is still used in the school system and many of the general populace are familiar with at least some of its poems.

Luo Binwang (619-684)

Luo Binwang was raised in Shandong. He served in court and over the years, penning many criticisms, often ran into problems and was banished and jailed. Notably, he criticized Empress Wu. He likely perished in the rebellion against her. His rediscovered tomb is now the sole tourist attraction in Yiwu County.

Luo was one of the Four Eminences of the Early Tang, although, unlike the others who were forerunners to later developments and aimed for a simpler style, he maintained complexity and allusiveness in his Old Style verse (*gushi*). But he did move away from Palace-Poetry themes dealing more with self-expression. He is most famous for composing the appealing "Ode to a Goose" at age seven (Chinese-style age). He was also an excellent prose writer.

Ode to a Goose

Goose, goose, goose,
neck bent, you sing to the sky.
White-feathered, you swim on green waters,
webbed red feet paddling back clear waves.

Luo Binwang (640-684)

詠鵝

鵝 鵝 鵝
曲項向天歌
白毛浮綠水
紅掌撥清波

駱賓王

Du Shenyan (645-708)

Du Shenyan was born in what is now Hubei. He was court poet to Empress Wu but later was exiled to the western frontier. He was recalled and assumed the role of tutor to the heir-apparent. He died with honors. He was grandfather to the famous poet, Du Fu.

Only about forty of his poems survive. One group reflects his time at court and are overly formal. The other dates from the time of his exile and have a freer and more personal expression. His most famous poem, included in *300 Tang Poems* is "Travelling And Viewing The Landscape In Early Spring."

Travelling and Viewing the Landscape in Early Spring: In Reply to Deputy Magistrate Lu of Jinling County (A Poem after Wen Yingwu)

There is an official, travelling alone,
who, oddly enough, is startled by the change of season.
Rose-tinted clouds rise over the sea at dawn;
crossing the spring river, plum trees and willows can be seen.
The pleasant weather quickens the golden orioles;
clear light flickers off the waterclover.
Suddenly I hear you sing an ancient song;
thoughts of longing to go home – tears wet my handkerchief.

Du Shenyan (645-708)

和晉陵陸丞早春游望（一作韋應物詩）

獨有宦游人，
偏驚物候新。
雲霞出海曙，
梅柳渡江春。
淑氣催黃鳥，
晴光轉綠蘋。
忽聞歌古調，
歸思欲沾巾。

杜審言

Chen Zi’ang (656-698 or 661-702)

Chen came from Sichuan. His official career was slow but solid. However, returning home on his father’s death, he was persecuted by the local magistrate on orders from Empress Wu’s cousin, whom he had criticized, and died.

Chen advocated a return to deep feelings and serious themes in poetry, as well as a simpler style, in reaction to the previous Palace-Style poetry. He is best known for his collection of thirty-eight poems *Moved by my Experiences* (*ganyu*), which have a distinct Daoist flavor. These poems were allegorical criticisms against Empress Wu and the government, but that meaning was lost by the end of the Tang and the poems were read for their surface meaning. It took later critics to revive the original meaning.

A Song on Youzhou Tower

I have not seen the ancient men who came before me;
I shall not see those who will come after me.
Thinking of the endless ages of heaven and earth,
I grieve alone and my tears fall.

Chen Zi'ang (656-698 or 661-702)

登幽州台歌

前不見古人，
后不見來者。
念天地之悠悠，
獨愴然而涕下。

陳子昂

Zhang Ruoxu (660-720)

Little is known about Zhang Ruoxu. He did have a minor military post at one point in his career. Along with He Zhizhang he achieved fame as one of a group of four poets from the Lower Yangtze Basin known as the "Four Scholars from Wuzhong." Only two of his poems survive. His old style, seven-character line verse, "A Night of Blossoms and Moonlight on the River in Spring" broke from previous conventions, depicting the sorrows of the common people.

A Night of Blossoms and Moonlight on the River in Spring: A Poem Written in Reply to a Lyric on Leave-Taking

In springtime, the river tide
merges level with the sea.
Over the ocean, a bright moon
rises with the tide,
shimmering on the waves
as far as the eye can see.
Where on the spring river
is there a place with no moonlight?

The river flows
winding and twisting through fragrant fields;
The moon shines on the blossoming trees;
it looks like sleet.
There seems to be an invisible frost
floating in the air;
The white sands on riverbank
appear to vanish.

The sky and river are of one hue,
without a speck of dust;
Bright, bright in the sky,
the solitary moon rolls on.
From this riverbank,
who first saw the moon?
Over this river, when did the moon
first shine on people?

Generation after generation, people are born
without end;
year after year, gaze at the river's moon,
the same.
I wonder who it is
the river moon is waiting for?
I only see the Yangtze River,

its flowing waters on their way.

A single white cloud
slowly drifts by;
Green-leafed maples are on the riverbank –
the sadness is unbearable.
To whose home will the small boat go
tonight?
On what moonlit tower
is she longing for him?

How moving! Above the tower
the moon lingers on;
it must be shining on the dressing table
of the woman left behind.
She cannot shut it out by rolling it up
in her chamber's white blinds;
Brushing it off her fulling block,
it always returns.

At this moment, we both gaze
but cannot hear one another.
I wish to follow the moon
and flow with its light to you.
Swan geese fly far
but they cannot pass the light.
Fishes and dragons dive and leap in the water,
creating ripples.

Last night, by the still pool,
I dreamed of fallen blossoms.
It's pitiful, spring is half over
and I haven't gone back home.
Spring, flowing away with the river's waters,
is almost at an end.
The moon once more, is setting in the west
over Yangtze's pools.

The moon slants and sinks, hidden by a mist
over the sea.
The road between Jieshu Mountain and the Xiang River
is without end.
I don't know how many people are returning home,
taking advantage of this moonlight.
The moon, setting over the river and trees,
stirs my heart to the brim.

Zhang Ruoxu (660-720)

相和歌辭•春江花月夜

春江潮水連海平，
海上明月共潮生。
灩灩隨波千萬里，
何處春江無月明。

江流宛轉繞芳甸，
月照花林皆似霰。
空里流霜不覺飛，
汀上白沙看不見。

江天一色無纖塵。
皎皎空中孤月輪。
江畔何人初見月，
江月何年初照人。

人生代代無窮已，
江月年年望相似。
不知江月待何人，
但見長江送流水。

白雲一片去悠悠，
青楓浦上不勝愁。

誰家今夜扁舟子，
何處相思明月樓。

可憐樓上月裴回，
應照離人妝鏡台。
玉戶簾中卷不去，
搗衣砧上拂還來。

此時相望不相聞，
願逐月華流照君。
鴻雁長飛光不度，
魚龍潛躍水成文。

昨夜閑潭夢落花，
可憐春半不還家。
江水流春去欲盡，
江潭落月復西斜。

斜月沉沉藏海霧，
碣石瀟湘無限路。
不知乘月几人歸，
落月搖情滿江樹。

張若虛

Zhang Jiuling (678-740)

Zhang came from then remote Guangdong. He came from a noted family, although it had declined somewhat. However, having placed second in the imperial examinations (*jinshi*), he gained official position and steadily rose to the role of Chancellor. He carried out his duties admirably and was esteemed by Emperor Xuanzong, but he did have his enemies and there was a slight setback towards the end of his career. But he still fulfilled important duties until the day he died.

Most of his two hundred and fifty surviving poems use the five-character line and depict natural scenery of the south. He uses detailed descriptions and parallelism. His vocabulary is learned but not too abstruse. With Meng Haoran, he heralded in the High Tang period of poetry.

Being Moved to Write Twelve Poems: #1

Orchid leaves are luxuriant in spring;
cassia blossoms are sheer brilliance in autumn.
Flourishing in this vitality
that of itself generates the sublime seasons.
Who knows the forest-dwellers,
who listen to the breezes and sit together in delight?
Plants have their 'original nature';
what need for a beautiful woman to pluck them?

Zhang Jiuling (678-740)

感遇十二首・其一

蘭葉春葳蕤，
桂華秋皎潔。
欣欣此生意，
自爾為佳節。
誰知林棲者，
聞風坐相悅。
草木有本心，
何求美人折。

張九齡

Being Moved to Write Twelve Poems: #4

A solitary swan goose comes from over the sea,
not daring to look back at the ponds and lakes.
By his side, he sees a pair of kingfishers
who nest in the three-pearl tree.
Heroic atop the treasure tree,
must they not fear the crossbow pellets?
In their gaudy attire, they worry about people pointing;
cleverness brings on the hatred of the gods.
Now I am travelling in obscurity;
who would want to shoot me and where?

Zhang Jiuling (678-740)

感遇十二首・其四

孤鴻海上來，
池潢不敢顧。
側見雙翠鳥，
巢在三珠樹。
矯矯珍木巔，
得無金丸懼？
美服患人指，
高明逼神惡。
今我游冥冥，
弋者何所慕！

張九齡

Gazing at the Moon and Cherishing One Far Away

Above the sea, the bright moon rises;
at the horizon we share this moment.
In the evening, close friends resent being far apart;
All night, thoughts of you arise.
I put out the candle to enjoy the full brightness;
put on a coat as I feel the dew increasing.
I can't hand you a present,
so I'll go back to sleep and dream of our reunion.

Zhang Jiuling (678-740)

望月懷遠

海上生明月，
天涯共此時。
情人怨遙夜，
竟夕起相思。
滅燭憐光滿，
披衣覺露滋。
不堪盈手贈，
還寢夢佳期。

張九齡

Wang Zhihuan (688-744)

Wang was born in Shanxi. He held minor government posts and did not seem to be ambitious in this regard. Only six of his poems survive. He wrote in the regular quatrain mode. His “Ascending Stork Tower” and “Liangzhou Songs” are famous, the former with a philosophical slant and the latter perhaps allegorical. In the Tang he was best known for his frontier poetry. He is the subject of a popular story about being in a tavern where there were entertainers, with two fellow-poets, who were pleased that the first two songs were their work. But the “star performer” came on and sang Wang’s poem putting to rest “who was best”.

Ascending Stork Tower

The bright sun sets on the mountain crest;
the Yellow River flows to the sea.
Yearning to see a thousand miles,
I ascend one more stage of the tower.

Wang Zhihuan (688-744)

登鸛雀樓

白日依山盡
黃河入海流
欲窮千里目
更上一層樓

王之渙

Liangzhou[5] Songs: Two Poems

I

In the distance, white clouds
rise above the Yellow River.
A solitary city and mountains,
thousands of feet high.
Why must the Qiang flute[6]
bewail the willows?
The spring scenery does not cross
Jade Gate Pass[7].

II

Alone in the north, I gaze
at the massive clouds of dust.
Sometimes a slaughtered horse is raised to the alter
as a sacrifice.
The Han emperors are now
martial gods.
I cannot consent to return home
to my beloved.

Wang Zhihuan (688-742)

涼州詞二首

黃河遠上白雲間，
一片孤城萬仞山。
羌笛何須怨楊柳，
春光不度玉門關。

5 Located in the remote north-western region.
6 A vertical flute of the Qiang people.
7 A Great Wall pass leading to remote north and west regions.

單於北望拂雲堆，
殺馬登壇祭几回。
漢家天子今神武，
不肯和親歸去來。

王之渙

Meng Haoran (689-740)

Meng Haoran came from present-day Hubei province. He had an unsuccessful official career, failing the imperial examinations (*jinshi*) at age thirty-nine and not receiving an appointment until 737, which lasted less than a year.

Meng was a major poet who ushered in the High Tang with Zhang Jiuling (who in fact, gave him his one and only official position). He was the elder friend of Wang Wei and Li Bai. He wrote many poems regarding his native place and even lived for a brief time as a recluse at Deer Gate Mountain. His nature poems tend to be detailed and descriptive but even in these his personality imbues the poetry.

Spring Dawn

Springtime, still asleep, I was unaware dawn had come.
I hear birds chirping everywhere.
During the night there was the sound of wind and rain –
I wonder how many blossoms have fallen.

Meng Haoran (689-740)

春曉

春眠不覺曉
處處聞啼鳥
夜來風雨聲
花落知多少

孟浩然

Qiwu Qian (692-749)

Qiwu was a born in what is modern Hubei. He passed the imperial examinations in 726 and associated with other poets in Chang'an including Wang Wei, who addressed a poem to him. His work is objective and technically well done. Slightly over twenty of his poems are extant with one group being on partings and the other on Daoist and Buddhist temples. Both themes are common motifs of the era.

Drifting on Ruoye Stream in Spring

My resolve for seclusion remains unbroken;
here I just aimlessly drift about.
The evening breeze blows my boat along
through a trail of flowers, entering the mouth of a stream.
At nightfall I turn west into a ravine;
I gaze at the Southern Dipper beyond the mountains.
The mist over a pool moves and swirls about;
the moon begins to set behind the wood.
Worldly affairs are overwhelming;
I just wish to be an old man, fishing pole in hand.

Qiwu Qian (692-749)

春泛若耶溪

幽意無斷絕，
此去隨所偶。
晚風吹行舟，
花路入溪口。
際夜轉西壑，
隔山望南斗。
潭煙飛溶溶，
林月低向后。
生事且彌漫，
願為持竿叟。

綦毋潛

Qiu Wei (694-789?)

Qiu was the longest living Tang poet of note (and likely including other dynasties as well). He was an official and retired at age 80, returning to his hometown. He was known, besides his poetry, for his filial piety to his stepmother. He was grouped with the Field and Garden (*tianyuan*) poetry in the tradition of Tao Yuanming. Wang Wei and Liu Zongyuan were among his friends and the former wrote a poem addressed to him. Qiu also had affiliations with Chan monks. He usually wrote poetry in the five-character line form, about nature and reclusion, his philosophy informed by Chan Buddhism.

Seeking the Recluse of West Mountain but not Meeting Him

At the very peak, a thatched hut,
thirty *li*[8] straight up.
Knock on the door, there's no houseboy;
peep in the room, there's only a small table.
If he's not out in his covered cart,
he must be fishing in the autumn waters.
Inadvertently, we don't see each other;
I've strived in vain to pay my respects.
The color of grass in the recent rain;
the soughing of pines through the window:
having made it here, this reclusive spot infuses me;
in itself, it cleanses my listening heart.
Though we have not played guest and host as I wished,
I have thoroughly attained the principle of purity.
Having fulfilled my intentions, I head down the mountain.
What need to wait for him?

Qiu Wei (694-789?)

尋西山隱者不遇

絕頂一茅茨，
直上三十里。
扣關無僮仆，
窺室惟案几。
若非巾柴車，
應是釣秋水。
差池不相見，

8 About a third of a mile

黽勉空仰止。
草色新雨中，
松聲晚窗里。
及玆契幽絕，
自足蕩心耳。
雖無賓主意，
頗得清淨理。
興盡方下山，
何必待之子？

邱為

Wang Changling (698-756)

Wang Changling was born in Chang'an, the Tang dynasty capital. He passed the imperial examinations (*jinshi*), but never held an important post. He was once banished to Guangdong but later recalled and appointed administrator of Jiangning. Later he was executed by a jealous Tang official during the An Lushan Rebellion.

Wang was highly rated in his time. He wrote a number of Frontier Poetry pieces and many are in the *yuefu* style. He excelled in both five- and seven-character line poetry. He was friends with Wang Wei and Li Bai. A little less than two hundred of his poems survive. He also wrote an important critical work, *Rules of Poetry*, which was lost in China but partly preserved in the writings of the Japanese monk, Kukai. It focuses on the psychological aspects of creative work.

Gazing at the Moon in the South Study with my Cousin Xiao and Remembering Cui of Shanyun County, Shaoxing

We take our ease in the south study;
through the open screen the moon begins to rise.
It's pure radiance reflects dimly off the trees by the water
and ripples through the window.
How often has it slowly waxed and waned,
transparent, the transformation of present to past?
That fine person is by the clear Yangtse's side;
In the evening, Yue chants are hard to bear.
But what's a thousand miles?
A breeze blows through the orchids and wild pear.

Wang Changling (698-756)

同從弟銷南齋玩月憶山陰崔少府

高臥南齋時，
開帷月初吐。
清輝淡水木，
演漾在窗戶。
苒苒几盈虛，
澄澄變今古。
美人清江畔，
是夜越吟苦。
千里其如何，
微風吹蘭杜。

王昌齡

Chang Jian (early 8th century)

Chang Jian was raised in Chang'an and passed the imperial examinations (*jinshi*) in 727. He only held minor provincial posts and retired to the countryside, living a life of seclusion.

He is noted for frontier and recluse poetry and fewer than sixty of his poems survive. However they show a great variety and originality. Two of his poems were included in *300 Tang Poems,* one of which deals with his stay at Wang Changling's retreat.

Behind the Meditation Hall of Po Mountain Temple

A clear day dawns on the grounds of this ancient temple
as the sun lights up the woods on high.
A path through bamboo leads to this secluded spot –
the meditation hall lies deep amongst flowering trees.
The bright mountain delights the birds;
the pool reflects one's emptied mind.
The ten thousand sounds are silent here
but for the tolling of the temple bell.

Chang Jian (early 6th century)

題破山寺后禪院

清晨入古寺，
初日照高林。
曲徑通幽處，
禪房花木深。
山光悅鳥性，
潭影空人心。
萬籟此俱寂，
惟余鐘磬音。

常建

Going to Visit Li the Ninth on Shangsi Festival[9]

There is a pause in the rain
　　at the ferry-landing east of the willow woods;
everlasting harmony on the Double Third,
　　I row my light boat.
The house of my old friend
　　is on Peach Blossom bank;
straight to its gates
　　the stream's waters flow.

Chang Jian (early 6th century)

三日尋李九莊

雨歇楊林東渡頭，
永和三日蕩輕舟。
故人家在桃花岸，
直到門前溪水流。

常建

9 Festival held on the third day of the third month

Wang Wei (701-761)

Wang Wei is one of the three greatest Tang poets, with Du Fu and Li Bai, and one of the five greatest poets of China. He was also a talented musician and a famous landscape painter who influenced the development of this art. Although he always expressed the conflict between reclusion and office, he never really retired from office. He was devoted to Chan Buddhism, perhaps following in his mother's footsteps. Born Wang Mojie, he assumed the courtesy name Wei which together with Mojie was the transliteration of the name of the famous lay Buddhist figure Vimalakirti.

He came from a distinguished family in Shanxi. He passed the imperial examinations (*jinshi*) in 721 with high marks. His career had its ups and downs. After his wife died, he never remarried. He set up his Lantian estate outside of Chang'an. He spent some time on the frontier at Liangzhou. During the An Lushan Rebellion he was captured and later accused of collaborating with the enemy. However his brother intervened and producing a poem that showed his loyalty, secured his release. Afterwards, he died peacefully at his estate.

Wang was the inheritor of Tao Yuanming's Field and Stream poetry. Although he also wrote in the Landscape (*shansui*) mode, his descriptions are quite general and serve to present his Buddhist sensibility. However, we should not be too simplistic, and there were also Confucian and Daoist elements in his work. About four hundred of his works survive. Although noted as a poet of nature, many of his poems deal with other matters, such as leave-takings, court poetry and so on. His most famous poems include "Deer Park" and the *Wang River Sequence* with his friend Pei Di about various sites on his Lantian estate.

Bamboo Pavilion

Alone in the secluded bamboo grove,
playing the zither and whistling along;
no one knows someone is deep in the woods
where the bright moon comes and shines.

Wang Wei (701-761)

竹里館

獨坐幽篁里
彈琴復長嘯
深林人不知
明月來相照

王維

Deer Park

Empty mountains
you can see no one,
only hear
echoes of voices.
Evening sun again
penetrates the forest floor
illuminating
glistening green moss.

Wang Wei (701-762)

鹿柴

空山不見人,
但聞人語響.
返景入深林,
復照青苔上.

王維

Visiting Accumulated Fragrance Temple

I am not familiar with Xiangji Temple;
I journey several miles through cloudy peaks.
Among ancient trees, no one is on the path;
from where does the bell sound deep in the mountains?
A brook gurgles amidst dangerous rocks;
the green pines seem chilled in the sun's rays.
At dusk by the bend of a still pond
peaceful meditation restrains the poison dragon.

Wang Wei (701-762)

過香積寺

不知香積寺
數里入雲峰。
古木無人徑
深山何處鐘？
泉聲咽危石
日色冷青松。
薄暮空潭曲
安禪制毒龍，

王維

Li Bai (701-762)

Li Bai is one of China's greatest poets. He grew in what is now Sichuan and purportedly his poetry shows a strident poetic voice that is associated with the region (see also Su Shi). In youth, he wandered Daoist-like, yet also seeking patrons. A Daoist practitioner with court ties aided him in getting a posting, outside the usual channels, at the court of Emperor Xuanzong. Given his drinking and eccentric behavior, he was expelled a couple of years later and wandered the south-east looking for patronage and complained that his genius was being neglected ("The Banished Immortal"). He got caught up in the An Lushan Rebellion and was arrested for treason, but late released. He then wandered the Yangtze until his death. He had married four times. A spurious story of his death states that, while drunk in a boat, he tried to embrace the reflection of the moon in the water, and fell in and drowned.

Li Bai's surviving poetry amounts to somewhat more than a thousand pieces, although some may not in fact be his. He wrote about sixty poems in Old Style verse with Confucian themes. He also wrote *yuefu* using various persona, and songs that were similar, but expressed his own thoughts and feelings. Most of his poems were occasional pieces. Some of these were conventional, some attained a supreme simplicity and others were seemingly dashed off. His personal poems in this category include his most famous, such as "Drinking Alone beneath the Moon." Many of his poems are extremely imaginative. He was friends with Du Fu, who valued him highly. There is some question as to how much he reciprocated. Although he did make an impression in his lifetime, like Du Fu, he only started to gain a high reputation in mid-Tang and it went up from there. Even in his fantastic poems, he retains a simplicity and feeling of spontaneity while much of his diction is colloquial. Much later, he was to influence Modernist poetics in America.

Diversions

There's wine across from me; I wasn't aware it was dark;
fallen blossoms cover my clothes.
Drunk, I rise and walk by a moonlit stream;
the birds have returned but people are few.

Li Bai (701-762)

自遣

對酒不覺暝，
落花盈我衣。
醉起步溪月，
鳥還人亦稀。

李白

Drinking Alone beneath the Moon

Among the blossoms, a jug of wine,
I drink alone as no close friends are near.
I raise my cup and invite the moon;
my shadow opposite makes three.
But the moon knows not how to drink,
and shadow can only follow my body.
For now the moon and shadow are my companions –
let’s enjoy and make the most of spring!
I sing, the moon moves about;
I dance, my shadow skitters helter-skelter.
While I’m sober, together we’ll be friends;
afterwards when I’m drunk, we’ll each go our own way.
Forever connected, beyond emotion as we drift,
we’ll meet later in the distant Milky Way.

Li Bai (701-762)

月下獨酌四首

花間一壺酒，
獨酌無相親。
舉杯邀明月，
對影成三人。
月既不解飲，
影徒隨我身。
暫伴月將影，
行樂須及春。
我歌月裴回，
我舞影零亂。
醒時同交歡，
醉后各分散。
永結無情游，
相期邈雲漢。

李白

Holding a Cup of Wine and Reflecting on the Moon

There's a moon in the blue sky;
 when did it come there?
I'll put my cup down right now
 and ask it.
People want to climb to the bright moon
 but can't.
The moon travels along
 but lags behind people.

Bright like a flying mirror, it glides
 over the vermilion gate-towers.
When the green mist dissipates completely,
 it sends forth a pure radiance.
We only see it at night
 rising above the sea.
How do we know that at dawn,
 it will sink amidst the clouds?

The white rabbit[10] pounds his medicine;
 autumn turns to spring.
Chang-e dwells alone;
 who is her neighbour?
Present-day people do not see the moon
 of ancient times.
But today's moon has shone
 on people of ancient times.

Ancient people, present-day people,
 are like flowing water –
Together, in seeing the bright moon,
 they are all alike.

10 The rabbit is the one on the moon in Chinese mythology. Chang'e is goddess of the moon.

I only wish to be in the realm of song
with wine across from me,
and moonlight forever shining
into my golden goblet.

Li Bai (701-762)

把酒問月

青天有月來几時，
我今停杯一問之：
人攀明月不可得，
月行卻與人相隨？

皎如飛鏡臨丹闕，
綠煙滅盡清輝發？
但見宵從海上來，
寧知曉向雲間沒？

白兔搗藥秋復春，
嫦娥孤棲與誰鄰？
今人不見古時月，
今月曾經照古人。

古人今人若流水，
共看明月皆如此。
唯願當歌對酒時，
月光長照金樽里。

李白

Listening to the Sichuan Monk Jun Play the Zither

The Sichuan monk cradles his zither,
out in the west under Mt. Emei’s peak.
For me, a sweep of his hand –
it’s like listening to the pines of ten thousand valleys.
This guest’s heart is cleansed with flowing water;
the sound mingles with that of the chill temple bell.
I am unaware that twilight has set on the emerald mountains;
how many layers of autumn clouds are concealed in the darkness?

Li Bai (701-762)

聽蜀僧浚彈琴

蜀僧抱綠綺，
西下峨眉峰；
為我一揮手，
如聽萬壑松。
客心洗流水，
余響入霜鐘。
不覺碧山暮，
秋雲暗几重？

李白

Question and Answer from the Mountains

You ask the meaning
        of my living in the jade green mountains.
I'll laugh but not answer;
        my heart of itself is calm.
Peach blossoms on the flowing streams
        go to the mysterious deep;
there is another heaven and earth
        not of the human world.

Li Bai (701-762)

山中問答

問余何意棲碧山,
笑而不答心自閑.
桃花流水窅然去,
別有天地非人間.

李白

Thoughts in Spring

Yan grass is like green silk threads;
Qin mulberries droop on green branches.
All day the gentleman longs to return;
meanwhile, the concubine is heartbroken.
Spring breeze – we don't know each other;
what business do you have, blowing in through my silk curtains?

Li Bai (701-762)

春思

燕草如碧絲，
秦桑低綠枝。
當君懷歸日，
是妾斷腸時。
春風不相識，
何事入羅幃。

李白

Thoughts On A Quiet Night

Before my bed, bright moonlight;
it looks like frost on the ground.
I lift my head and gaze at the bright moon;
I lower my head, full of thoughts of my home town.

Li Bai (701-762)

靜夜思

床前明月光
疑是地上霜
舉頭望明月
低低思故鄉

李白

Liu Zhangqing (709-785)

Liu Zhangqing came from a distinguished family in Hebei province. He passed the imperial examinations (*jinshi)* in 733 and held official posts in the provinces, including governor of Suizhou in 780. However, like most, his career had its ups and downs and he imprisoned, then demoted twice. Finally he was banished and then dismissed from office.

More than five hundred of his poems survive. Many are occasional pieces of little interest but he wrote a number of landscape poems in five-character verse, influenced by Tao Yuanming and Wang Wei, which are highly regarded.

Passing by Piao Mu's[11] Tomb

The worthy of ancient times cherished a single meal;
but that ended a thousand autumns ago.
The woodcutters know her ancient tomb;
the waters of the ancient kingdom of Chu flow on.
Waterclover along the banks provides a mat for the traveller;
mountains and trees allay the cuckoo's sadness.
The spring grasses are green and vast,
here, where the prince of old roamed.

Liu Changqing (709-785)

經漂母墓

昔賢懷一飯，
玆事已千秋。
古墓樵人識，
前朝楚水流。
渚蘋行客荐，
山木杜鵑愁。
春草茫茫綠，
王孫舊此游。

劉長卿

11 An old woman who aided Han Xin (231 BC-196 BC) in his youth

Seeing Off The Monk Lingche

The Bamboo Grove Temple is gray in the haze;
the bell in the distance can just be heard.
The bamboo hat on your back, bears the setting sun;
alone, you return home to the distant green mountains.

Liu Changqing (709-785)

送靈澈上人

蒼蒼竹林寺
杳杳鐘聲晚
荷笠帶斜陽
青山獨歸遠

劉長卿

Seeking the Daoist Living in Seclusion at Nanxi on Changshan Mountain

All the way, at the places I pass through,
I see footprints in the moss.
White clouds hover over tranquil islets;
spring grass obstructs your idle gate.
The rain ended, I see the color of the pines;
I follow up the mountain to the stream's source.
The flowers by the brook and your meditating mind
face each other – I am at a loss for words.

Liu Zhangqing (709-785)

尋南溪常山道人隱居

一路經行處，
莓苔見屐痕。
白雲依靜渚，
春草閉閑門。
過雨看松色，
隨山到水源。
溪花與禪意，
相對亦忘言。

劉長卿

Du Fu (712-770)

If one had to choose the outstanding Chinese poet then it would likely be Du Fu. His family was distinguish but in decline. His grandfather was the poet Du Shenyan. Du Fu failed the imperial examinations (*jinshi*) twice, before passing in 751. He had become friends with Li Bai in 744. He was offered his first position in 755 but it was not promising and he declined. Just as he became associated with the heir apparent, the An Lanshu Rebellion broke out, the emperor abdicated and the heir apparent became emperor. Du Fu attempted to join the new emperor but was captured and imprisoned for a year before his escape. He obtained a court position thereafter but was involved in some controversy and exiled to Huazhou. He then resigned, going to Chengdu with his family. But he had to move often in these later years and while wandering down the Yangtze during the last three years of his life, he died.

Much of Du Fu's poetry has been lost because of his wanderings and because his greatness was not recognized in his time, partly due to his innovations. However, close to fifteen hundred poems remain, mostly from the latter part of his life. In his early poetry, prior to going to Chang'an in 746, he already showed a tendency to transcend genre and use startling juxtapositions. In his second period, 746-759, Du Fu further dissolved the boundaries of poetic genres. He also treated non-poetic topics and thus we have, for example, poems addressed by name to his servants. He could also employ a plain or elaborate style. His final period encompassed his years of wandering subsequent to the An Lanshu Rebellion. Most of his poems survive from this period and they include his most famous, showing a move to further technical difficulty, and eventually influencing the Late Tang poets. His "Autumn Meditations" from this period is one of his finest works.

As mentioned previously, Du Fu was not greatly appreciated in his time. However, throughout the Tang, his reputation grew and by the Song dynasty he had been elevated to the highest status and became an emulated poet for centuries to follow. Du Fu's poems are mainly Confucian in sensibility and a profound humaneness shines out in poems on others or about himself, whether about the joys or sorrows of life.

Dharma Mirror Temple[12]

My life endangered I fled to another prefecture;
I strove my utmost but had to end my strenuous efforts.
My spirit wounded, I went deep into the mountains;
my worries vanished at this ancient clifftop temple.

The pure green lichens sparkle.
Fallen leaves seem woeful; cold bamboo sheaths huddle together.
A river winds at the foot of the mountain;
gradually the pines get wet from the rain above.
Dispersing clouds obscure the clear morning;
the rising sun is hidden then bursts through.
The vermilion rafters glow in the partial light;
doors and windows gleam everywhere.

I lean on my staff forgetting earlier events;
emerging from the ground pines, it's already noon.
Through the gloom a cuckoo calls;
I dare not take the narrow path again.

Du Fu (712-770)

法鏡寺

身危適他州，
勉強終勞苦。
神傷山行深，
愁破崖寺古。
嬋娟碧鮮淨，
蕭摵寒籜聚。
回回山根水，
冉冉松上雨。

12 Fajing Temple

泄雲蒙清晨，
初日翳復吐。
朱甍半光炯，
戶牖粲可數。
拄策忘前期，
出蘿已亭午。
冥冥子規叫，
微徑不復取。

杜甫

Full Moon

The lonely moon above the tower is full;
the cold Yangtse flows by my door in the night.
Cast on the waves, the gold reflection wavers;
illuminated, my mat outshines silk.
Lacking nothing, the empty mountains are peaceful,
reaching high where constellations are sparse.
In my ancient garden pines and cassia trees flourish;
spreading ten thousand miles we share pure radiance.

Du Fu (712-770)

月圓

孤月當樓滿，
寒江動夜扉。
委波金不定，
照席綺逾依。
未缺空山靜，
高懸列宿稀。
故園松桂發，
萬里共清輝。

杜甫

Moonlit Night

Tonight, the moon is over Fuzhou;
in your chamber, you can only gaze at it alone.
So distant, I pity our children
who do not understand “memories of Chang’an”.
A fragrant mist dampens your hair;
the brightness shines cold on your beautiful arms.
When shall we lean by the open curtain,
the moonlight upon us, all traces of our tears dried?

Du Fu (712-770)

月夜

今夜鄜州月，
閨中只獨看。
遙憐小兒女，
未解憶長安。
香霧雲鬟溼，
清輝玉臂寒。
何時倚虛幌，
雙照淚痕干。

杜甫

Stars and Moon by the Yangtse #1

A sudden shower cleanses the autumn night;
golden waves reflect the brilliant white cord –
the Milky Way's pristine brightness.
The Yangtze riverside has always been clear.
Reflected, the connected chain wavers and sunders;
at the horizon, the mirror moon rises.
The fading light is dimmed even more by the water-clock
as dew begins to condense on the flowers.

Du Fu (712-770)

江邊星月

驟雨清秋夜，
金波耿玉繩。
天河元自白，
江浦向來澄。
映物連珠斷，
緣空一鏡升。
余光隱更漏，
況乃露華凝。

杜甫

The Seagulls

By the river's edge the cold gulls play,
they do nothing other than as they please.
Changing their minds they turn their jade-white wings;
following a whim they dot the green field of sprouting rice.

In the darkening snow they must return to bathe.
When the wind arises they just drift along.
Two or three flocks hover over the blue sea,
sunlit images uttering wailful cries.

Du Fu (712-768)

鷗

江浦寒鷗戲，
無他亦自饒。
卻思翻玉羽，
隨意點青苗。
雪暗還須浴，
風生一任飄。
几群滄海上，
清影日蕭蕭。

杜甫

Zhang Ji (713-779)

Zhang Ji was a scholar-poet from Xianzhou who passed the imperial examinations in 753 and held a number of regional and central government posts. His forty-odd poems are not well known, and he is not considered a leading poet of the Tang dynasty. Many of his poems concern his feelings on visiting famous sites or scenic spots. Other poems have a more philosophic bent. However it is his "Moored by the Maple Bridge at Night" that has garnered him lasting fame.

Night Mooring by Maple Bridge

The moon descends and crows call out
 in the frost-filled sky;
Maples and fishermen's fires by the banks
 lie opposite; my sleep is fitful.
Outside Gusu City
 sits Cold Mountain Temple;
At midnight, the tolling of its bells
 resounds unto my boat.

Zhang Ji (713-779)

楓橋夜泊

月落烏啼霜滿天，
江楓漁火對愁眠。
姑蘇城外寒山寺，
夜半鐘聲到客船。

張繼

Zhang Xu (8th century)

Zhang is famous for his cursive calligraphy. He was a heavy drinker and associated with Li Bai. His "Peach Blossom Spring" appears in the famous anthology *300 Tang Poems*.

Peach Blossom Stream

Obscure, the flying bridge
through the back country mist.
By rocks overhanging the west bank
I ask a fishing boat,
"Peach blossoms all day long
follow the flowing waters;
on which side of the clear stream
is the cave?"

Zhang Xu (8th century)

桃花溪

隱隱飛橋隔野煙，
石磯西畔問漁船。
桃花盡日隨流水，
洞在清溪何處邊。

張旭

Sikong Shu (720-790)

Sikong was born in what is now Hebei. He had a successful, if undistinguished, career in office.

Sikong was one of the Ten Poetic Talents of the Dali Period (766-779). About one hundred and seventy poems survive. Some are of the Leave-taking genre and others express his feelings and thoughts. In fact, most of his poems are personal. His style tends to the simple, in both expression and theme. Three of his poems appear in *300 Tang Poems*.

The Stone Well

In spring, the color of moss covers all the rocks;
the shade of the paulownia enters the cold well.
When the solitary recluse draws water,
he first enjoys the rays of the setting sun.

Sikong Shu (720-790)

石井

苔色遍春石，
桐陰入寒井。
幽人獨汲時，
先樂殘陽影。

司空曙

Wei Yingwu (737-791)

Wei was born in Chang'an and came from a distinguished family. He served in the imperial guard of Emperor Xuanzong. He then held a number of positions in the capital area before being posted as a prefect in the south three times.

Being a follower of Tao Yuanming, his poems present tranquil natural settings in a simple language, usually using the five-character line. In this he was also influenced by Wang Wei. He did, though, also touch on social issues. Later poets associated him with Liu Zongyuan. Twelve of his poems appear in the *300 Tang Poems*.

Sent to a Daoist Priest in the Quanjiao Mountains

Today, it was cold at the prefecture office.
Suddenly I thought of you, dwelling in the mountains –
down by a stream, bundling up brambles for firewood;
then returning home to boil your white crystals.
I wanted to bring you a half-gourd of wine;
go all that distance to comfort you on this rainy, windy evening.
But fallen leaves cover the desolate mountains;
where would I seek your tracks.

Wei Yingwu (737-791)

寄全椒山中道士

今朝郡齋冷，
忽念山中客。
澗底束荊薪，
歸來煮白石。
欲持一瓢酒，
遠慰風雨夕。
落葉滿空山，
何處尋行跡。

韋應物

Lu Lun (739-799)

Lu Lun was born in what is now Shanxi. He tried several times, but never passed the imperial examinations (*jinshi*). He did manage to hold some important government posts, with the usual ups and downs, in the end being demoted.

Like Sikong Shu he was one of the Ten Poetic Talents of the Dali Period (766-779). He was skilled in the use of parallelism and realistic description. He wrote on a variety of subjects but the bulk was social poetry and occasional pieces written in five-character line Regulated Verse.

An Ancient Tree in the Mountains

The lofty tree is already bleak and desolate
from last night's rain and the autumn winds.
Its fallen leaves rustle in the bamboo grove
while its slanting roots snag tumbleweeds.
Half immersed in the mountain scenery,
it is constantly amidst the river's sound.
Whoever makes it to this place,
also passes through the gate of clouds.

Lu Lun (739-799)

山中詠古木

高木已蕭索，
夜雨復秋風。
墜葉鳴叢竹，
斜根擁斷蓬。
半侵山色里，
長在水聲中。
此地何人到，
雲門去亦通。

盧綸

Staying the Night at Stone Jar Temple

In the worship hall, the lanterns are cold;
    fireflies flit in the grass.
A thousand forests, ten thousand valleys,
    are still and silent.
Mist thickens and gathers over the waters
    where dragons and serpents lie hidden.
Dew moistens the empty mountain
    under the bright Milky Way.
In the haze and fog of dusk
    the world seems sad.
Under the tinted clouds of dawn
    I can see the royal city.
I turn back and take a good look at it,
    then weep.
The billows of the world's bitter sea,
    when will they be calm?

Lu Lun (739-799)

宿石甕寺

殿有寒燈草有螢，
千林萬壑寂無聲。
煙凝積水龍蛇蟄，
露溼空山星漢明。
昏靄霧中悲世界，
曙霞光里見王城。
回瞻相好因垂淚，
苦海波濤何日平。

盧綸

The Pond Behind Xingshan Temple

Outside the window, white cranes roost;
it's like I'm looking over Mirror Lake.
How many years has the moon shone on these trees?
How many times have these flowers blossomed for people?
There is a road by the sedge along the riverbank;
the mossy path is green, untarnished by dust.
I always wished that I could be allowed to remain
among these monks with this old body.

Lu Lun (739-799)

題興善寺后池

隔窗棲白鶴，
似與鏡湖鄰。
月照何年樹，
花逢几遍人。
岸莎青有路，
苔徑綠無塵。
永願容依止，
僧中老此身。

盧綸

Liu Fangping (742-779)

Liu Fangping was from Liaoning. He passed the imperial examinations (*jinshi*) at an early age, served in the military and held office, from which he resigned in his thirties to live as a recluse in Henan. As well as a poet, he was a noted painter.

His surviving poems number only twenty-six but they show a fine depiction of natural landscapes. He had a number of minor poet friends. Two of his poems were included in *300 Tang Poems*.

Grieving in Spring

Through the window screen the sun sets
and gradually it is dusk.
In her golden room no one sees
the tracks of her tears.
In the lonely empty courtyard
the longing of a spring evening.
Pear blossoms cover the ground
but she does not open her door.

Liu Fangping (742-779)

春怨

紗窗日落漸黃昏，
金屋無人見淚痕。
寂寞空庭春欲晚，
梨花滿地不開門。

劉方平

Harvesting Lotus Song

The sun sets on a clear day over the Yangtze;
beautiful slender women are singing the “Bramble Song”.
Used to gathering lotus from childhood,
there are fifteen taking advantage of the low tide.

Liu Fangping (742-779)

采蓮曲

落日晴江里，
荊歌艷楚腰。
采蓮從小慣，
十五即乘潮。

劉方平

Spring Snow

A blizzard envelops the spring breeze;
chaotically, the snowflakes swirl in the air.
That gentleman outside, looks like a flower,
as the snow slants eastward through Luoyang.

Liu Fangping (742-779)

春雪

飛雪帶春風，
裴回亂繞空。
君看似花處，
偏在洛陽東。

劉方平

Li Duan (743-782?)

Li Duan was born in Hebei. He was grandson to Li Xiaozhen and nephew to the poet Li Jiayu. He held officials posts, including Palace Library Editor, until his early death.

He was another of the Ten Poetic Talents of Dalian. He perhaps studied poetry with Jiaoran. He was compared unfavorably with Sikong Shu who excelled at antithesis. Li did write fine seven-character line poems for occasional verse and songs. Lu Lun wrote a farewell poem to Li Duan, “Seeing Off Li Duan”, which is included in *300 Tang Poems*.

Boudoir Feelings

The moon sinks and stars thin out,
 day is about to break.
The solitary lamp is not yet extinguished;
 dreams do not arise.
I wrap a cloak around my shoulders
 and gaze out the door.
I will not be angry when morning comes
 and the magpies joyously sing.

Li Duan (743-782?)

閨情

月落星稀天欲明，
孤燈未滅夢難成。
披衣更向門前望，
不忿朝來鵲喜聲。

李端

Wu Yuanheng (758-815)

Wu was born into an eminent family near Luoyang. He passed the imperial examinations (*jinshi*) and rose steadily in position to become Chancellor under Emperor Xuanzong. He was ambushed and assassinated while in office in 815.

Less than two hundred poems of Wu survive. He was very popular in his time but in the later period when his fame dwindled, many poems were lost. He wrote mainly five-character verse. In the poem translated, he reflects his homesickness through vivid concrete imagery.

Springtime Yearning

The willows are shady;
 it is clear after a light shower.
The remaining flowers have fallen;
 see the orioles glide.
In the evening the spring breeze
 blows fragrant dreams,
dreams that pursue
 the spring breeze back to Luoyang.

Wu Yuanheng (758-815)

春興

楊柳陰陰細雨晴，
殘花落盡見流鶯。
春風一夜吹香夢，
夢逐春風到洛城。

武元衡

Wang Jian (751?-830?)

Wang passed the imperial examinations (*jinshi*) in 775 and held various provincial posts throughout his career.

He was associated with Zhang Ji in the new yuefu movement and wrote many seven-character poems in this genre whose aim was the expression of moral values. He was noted in his time for his palace-style poetry of which over one hundred survive. Many of these poems are in the five-character line style with female persona lamenting their treatment by society. Wang also wrote poems using the less common six-character line. One of his poems is included in *300 Tang Poems*.

Gazing at The Moon on the Fifteenth Night: Sent to Secretary-General Du

In the courtyard the ground is white;
crows roost in the trees.
A cold dew silently
wets the cassia flowers.
This evening the moon is so bright,
all gaze at it.
I don't know in whose home
there could be thoughts of autumn.

Wang Jian (766?-831?)

十五夜望月寄杜郎中

中庭地白樹棲鴉，
冷露無聲溼桂花。
今夜月明人盡望，
不知秋思在誰家。

王建

Bai Juyi (772-846)

Bai Juyi was born in Henan and his father was a minor official. He had much of his upbringing outside the parental home and was a precocious child. He passed the imperial examinations (*jinshi*) in 800. Shortly afterwards he met Yuan Zhen who was to become a lifetime friend. They both dreamed of social reform but these dreams were never realized. Bai never achieved high office and was often critical of the government and when he protested Yuan Zhen's banishment, he himself was exiled from Chang'an, although he still held office. Later he steeped himself in Buddhism and spent his last years in Luoyang.

Bai helped popularize poetry in his time, and indeed was himself very popular and esteemed by all classes. He perhaps strove to achieve this as he often aimed for simple diction and clarity in his poems. He also made great efforts to have his poetry preserved, which accounts for the surviving number exceeding 2,800. He was especially taken up in Japan, where his works appear in the *Tale of Genji* and various anthologies. He is also the subject of a Noh play.

He was a leader of the new *yuefu* movement with social criticism and injustices expressed in many of these poems. He also excelled in regulated verse. His most famous poems are "The Song of Everlasting Sorrow" which deals with Emperor Xianzong and Yang Guifei, and "Song of the *Pipa*" about a once famous woman *pipa* (lute) player, fallen on hard times. Bai is one of the greatest of Chinese poets whose works easily cut across different cultures.

Eight Lyrics on the Willow Bough #8

People say willow leaves
look like knitted eyebrows.
Further, melancholy is like
drooping willow branches.
A willow branch can be pulled till it breaks
and one can be lead along until heartbroken.
And neither one,
has any hope.

Bai Juyi (772-846)

楊柳枝詞八首

人言柳葉似愁眉，
更有愁腸似柳絲。
柳絲挽斷腸牽斷，
彼此應無續得期。

白居易

For my Guests: Returning Home in the Evening and Gazing Back at Gushan Temple on West Lake

On a pine-treed island with willows by the shore
 sits Lotus Blossom Temple;
it's evening and we move our home-bound oars
 leaving the sacred isle.
Cumquat fruit droops
 after the heavy mountain rain;
palm leaves tremble
 in the cool river breeze.
Through the mist in the calm waves
 the blue void ripples.
When we land, please gentlemen, turn your heads and gaze
 at Penglai Isle[13] in the middle of the sea.

Bai Juyi (772-846)

西湖晚歸回望孤山寺贈渚客

柳湖松島連花寺
晚動歸橈出道場。
盧橘子低山雨重
棕櫚葉戰水風涼。
煙波澹蕩搖空碧
樓殿參差倚夕陽。
到岸請君回首望
蓬萊宮在海中央。

白居易

13 Island of the Immortals.

Fu: Saying Farewell on the Grasses of the Ancient Plain

Lush are the grasses on the plain;
each year they wither then flourish.
Wildfires cannot burn them up;
spring winds blow life into them again.
Far off, its scent pervades the ancient road;
on a clear day the greenness extends from wilderness to city walls.
Again, I see the young prince off,
the luxuriant grass suffused with the pangs of parting.

Bai Juyi (772-846)

賦得古原草送別

離離原上草，
一歲一枯榮。
野火燒不盡，
春風吹又生。
遠芳侵古道，
晴翠接荒城。
又送王孫去，
萋萋滿別情。

白居易

Peach Blossoms at Dalin Temple

Back in the city, in April,
          fragrant blooms are finished.
At this mountain temple, peach blossoms
          are just beginning to reach full bloom.
I’ve long regretted that spring passes,
          nowhere to be found.
I didn’t know it moves on
          and ends up coming here!

Bai Juyi (772-846)

大林寺桃花

人間四月芳菲盡
山寺桃花始盛開
長恨春歸無覓處
不知轉入此中來

白居易

Village Night

In the dark green frosted grass
insects sadly chirp;
south village, north village,
no one is out walking.
Alone outside my front gate,
I gaze over the fields at night.
Under the bright moonlight
buckwheat flowers seem like snow.

Bai Juyi (772-846)

村夜

霜草蒼蒼蟲切切，
村南村北行人絕。
獨出前門望野田，
月明蕎麥花如雪。

白居易

Liu Zongyuan (773-819)

Liu Zongyuan was born in Chang'an and rose quickly in office. On the death of the emperor in 805 he was sent to a minor provincial post in Henan for ten years. On his recall he was sent to Liuzhou in what is now Guangxi, then a very remote area, and died there.

He was esteemed as a prose writer and allied with Han Yu in this regard in espousing the clarity and utility of the Ancient Style Prose Movement. On his exile he began to write *fu* and landscape essays. His later prose writings are considered his finest.

About 180 of his poems survive. His poetry is considered relatively minor and overshadowed by his prose. However he wrote a number of fine pieces and "River Snow" is a classic and was often a theme for painting. His late poems are imbued with a Confucian, Daoist and Buddhist sensibility, foreshadowing Neo-Confucianism. He also wrote allegories and animal fables.

An Autumn Morning Walk through an Abandoned Village in South Gorge

It is the end of autumn – frost and dew lie heavy
as morning dawns. I go to a secluded valley
where yellow leaves cover a bridge over a stream.
In a desolate village are only ancient trees;
in the cold, the scattered flowers look forlorn.
A tiny hidden stream seems to end but flows on.
Already, I have long forgotten my calculating mind,
so why do I startle that deer.

Liu Zongyuan (773-819)

秋曉行南谷經荒村

杪秋霜露重，
晨起行幽谷。
黃葉覆溪橋，
荒村唯古木。
寒花疏寂曆，
幽泉微斷續。
機心久已忘，
何事驚麋鹿？

柳宗元

At Dawn I Visit Transcendental Master's Courtyard to Study Buddhist Sutras

I draw cold water from the well to rinse my teeth;
with a pure heart I brush the dust from my clothes.
Leisurely I carry a palm-leaf scripture
and walk out of the east study reading it.
No one understands how to seek the true source;
the world pursues absurd ways.
Leave behind words, aim for the profound;
cultivate your nature to perfect it.
The Buddhist monk's courtyard is serene;
the emerald moss penetrates the bamboo grove.
The sun is rising but fog and dew persist;
the pines shine green like hair ointment.
Tranquil, I leave words behind
and joyfully awaken, my mind sufficient unto itself.

Liu Zongyuan (773-819)

晨詣超師院讀禪經

汲井漱寒齒，
清心拂塵服。
閑持貝葉書，
步出東齋讀。
真源了無取，
妄跡世所逐。
遺言冀可冥，
繕性何由熟。
道人庭宇靜，
苔色連深竹。
日出霧露余，
青松如膏沐。
澹然離言說，
悟悅心自足。

柳宗元

Lyric on a Caged Goshawk

There is a chill sleet wind
        and a severe frost blows in.
Above, the goshawk strikes and wheels about
        in the light of dawn.
Clouds split, the mist disperses
        and a fragment of rainbow appears.
Like a clap of thunder and flash of lightning
        it skims a hilltop ridge.
With a whoosh, its vigorous feathers cut through
        thorns and brambles.
Below it seizes fox and hare
        then soars into the blue vastness.
Fur on its talons, blood on its beak,
        a hundred birds flee.
It stands alone peering in four directions,
        holding high its fierce head.
When scorching winds and humid summer heat
        suddenly arrive,
the feathers of its wings moult and fall. It is devastated
        and goes into hiding.
Wildcats and rodents in the grass
        are enough to worry it.
In a single night it looks around ten times,
        alarmed and distressed.
Still, it wishes for the clear autumn skies to return,
        when it will be set free,
toss off its myriad burdens,
        and soar amidst the clouds.

Liu Zongyuan (773-819)

籠鷹詞

悽風淅瀝飛嚴霜，
蒼鷹上擊翻曙光。
雲披霧裂虹蜺斷，
霹靂掣電捎平岡。
砉然勁翮翦荊棘，
下攫狐兔騰蒼茫。
爪毛吻血百鳥逝，
獨立四顧時激昂。
炎風溽暑忽然至，
羽翼脫落自摧藏。
草中狸鼠足為患，
一夕十顧驚且傷。
但願清商復為假，
拔去萬累雲間翔。

柳宗元

River Snow

A thousand mountains block the flight of birds;
people’s tracks vanish in the myriad paths.
In a lone boat, an old man, wearing straw coat and bamboo hat,
fishes alone on the cold river in the falling snow.

Liu Zongyuan (773-819)

江雪

千山鳥飛絕
萬徑人蹤滅
孤舟簑笠翁
獨釣寒江雪

柳宗元

The Old Fisherman

The old fisherman spends the night
by the western cliffs.
At dawn he draws water from the clear Xiang
and lights a fire of Chu bamboo.
The mist dissolves in the rising sun;
there is no one to be seen.
The beating of oars is the only sound
in the green of mountains and hills.
Looking back, he sees the horizon
merge with midstream;
Above the cliffs
clouds mindlessly chase one another.

Liu Zongyuan (773-819)

漁翁

漁翁夜傍西岩宿，
曉汲清湘燃楚竹。
煙銷日出不見人，
欸乃一聲山水綠。
回看天際下中流，
岩上無心雲相逐。

柳宗元

Jia Dao (779-843)

Jia was born in Hubei and joined a Buddhist order, likely Chan, at an early age. He met Han Yu in Luoyang in 810 and left the order, going to Chang'an with Han. He failed the imperial examinations (*jinshi*) several times and only received minor provincial postings from 837 until his death.

His poetry can be divided into two styles. First was the discursive mode written in old-style poetry (*gushi*), and lyric poetry in five-character regulated verse, these latter representing his best work, using parallelism and colloquial language. There is a Buddhist sensibility to his work. However, later poets, notable Su Shi, found his work limited. However Su Shi's elder contemporary, Ouyang Xiu, did appreciate Jia's evocations of hardships.

There is a famous story of how Jia met Han Yu that is worth repeating. Jia Dao was riding his donkey one day, composing a poem. He couldn't decide if one line read better "A monk is knocking at a door by moonlight" or "pushing at a door…" He was so caught up in this, he failed to give way to Prefect Han Yu's entourage. Arrested and brought before Han, he told how he was trying to decide between the two words. Han Yu thought about this for some time and finally said "knocking" is better. Subsequent to that, they became close friends.

Inscribed at Li Ning's Retreat

You live in idleness with few neighbors near;
a grassed-over path leads to your wild garden.
Birds nest in the pond-side trees;
beneath the moon, this monk knocks at your gate.
Crossing the bridge, I can make out countryside colors;
rocks seem to shift at the root of moving clouds.
For now I must leave but I'll be back;
I won't break my word to visit your retreat.

Jia Dao (779-843)

題李凝幽居

閑居少鄰并，
草徑入荒園。
鳥宿池邊樹，
僧敲月下門。
過橋分野色，
移石動雲根。
暫去還來此，
幽期不負言。

賈島

Visiting but not Finding the Recluse at Home

Beneath the pines I ask the boy,
who replies “Master has gone to gather herbs
alone up the mountain,
hidden by clouds, whereabouts unknown.”

Jia Dao (779-843)

尋隱者不遇

松下問童子
言師采藥去
只在此山中
雲深不知處

賈島

Wen Tingyun (812-870)

Wen Tingyun in Shanxi province. He came from a prominent family. He failed the imperial examinations (*jinshi*) many times. He did obtain some postings due to his connections. He later reached some prominence but was eventually demoted and died shortly thereafter. He was apparently arrogant, decadent and lived a dissolute lifestyle.

Wen's great contribution was to the *ci*, a lyric form of poetry with irregular line lengths. With his contemporary, Li Shangyin, he paved the way for Li Yu at the end of the Tang and eventually for Su Shi's major contributions in the Song dynasty. In Wen Tingyun's verse the subject matter dealt with romance and used exotic and sensuous imagery, and was, in general, rather complex. The general consensus is that his *ci* are technically excellent.

He also wrote about three hundred regular poems, using both the five- and seven-character line. These poems show a greater range of theme and diction that the *ci*. There was a wide variety of language and style as well.

Inscribed to Reclusive Scholar Lu at his Mountain Dwelling

At West Stream this visitor asked the woodcutter;
then afar I noticed my host's well kept home.
Ancient trees grew out of the old rocks;
the sandy bottom of the clear rapid stream could be seen.
A thousand peaks stood darkened by the rain;
a single path sloped up into the clouds.
At dusk crows glided and gathered;
the mountains were overflowing with buckwheat flowers.

Wen Tingyun (812-870)

題盧處士山居

西溪問樵客，
遙識楚人家。
古樹老連石，
急泉清露沙。
千峰隨雨暗，
一徑入雲斜。
日暮飛鴉集，
滿山蕎麥花。

溫庭筠

Jade Zither Lament

On my silver-colored bed's icy mat,
dreams are incomplete.
The blue sky is like water;
the night clouds thin.
Far off is the sound of wild geese
on their way to Xiao and Xiang[14].
On the Twelve Towers, the moon, by its very nature,
shines brightly.

Wen Tingyun (812-870)

瑤瑟怨

冰簟銀床夢不成，
碧天如水夜雲輕。
雁聲遠過瀟湘去，
十二樓中月自明。

溫庭筠

14 Two famous rivers and a scenic spot in Hunan province.

Li Shangyin (813-858)

Li Shangyin was born in modern-day Henan province. His father, a magistrate, died in 821 and he moved to Luoyang. In 837 he passed the imperial examinations (*jinshi*). He never achieved high rank, but had positions in both Chang'an and the provinces. He died while out of office in his hometown.

There are 598 extant poems. His poetry is noted for its difficulty, denseness, allusiveness, symbolism, and obscurity and helped set the trend for Late Tang poetry. He was famous for writing untitled poems that are mostly about love affairs. He also wrote personal and social poems in a conservative manner. Further, there were political poems and allegorical poems. He was the most important poet of the Late Tang and had a great influence on subsequent writers. There was, though, some reaction to his complex style in the Song dynasty.

Chang'e[15]

On the mica screen,
the dark shadows from the candle.
The Milky Way gradually descends
and the stars at dawn are faint.
Chang'e must regret
stealing the elixir of the immortals –
in the blue sky over the emerald seas
her heart reflected night after night.

Li Shangyin (813-858)

常娥

雲母屏風燭影深，
長河漸落曉星沈。
常娥應悔偷靈藥，
碧海青天夜夜心。

李商隱

15 Goddess of the moon

Fallen Blossoms

From the high pavilion the guest has unexpectedly gone;
in the small garden, blossoms fly helter-skelter.
They land in heaps on the winding path –
some blow into the distance in the sun's slanting rays.
Heartbroken, I cannot yet sweep them away;
straining my eyes I want him to return.
My young girl's heart turns toward the end of spring;
all I have achieved is my tear-stained robe.

Li Shangyin (813-858)

落花

高閣客竟去，
小園花亂飛。
參差連曲陌，
迢遞送斜暉。
腸斷未忍掃，
眼穿仍欲歸。
芳心向春盡，
所得是沾衣。

李商隱

Zhang Jie (836-905)

Little is known about Zhang Jie. He wrote most of his poems in seven-character regular verse His poems often express social concerns and one of his most famous poems is “Book Burning Pit.” He was also innovative and created a new form of poetry, known as "The Reformed Form." His contemporaries called him a "novelty poet." About twenty-six of his poems survive.

The Peach Blossom Source

Where the jagged cliffs lean together
　　is the entrance to the cave;
there an ancient entered
　　the immortals' source.
Under many blossoming trees
　　he encountered pearls and kingfishers;
Laozi's descendents
　　were in the midst of song.
Afterwards he doubted it all –
　　it was like the garden-keeper's dream[16];
returning home, who would believe
　　the words of an old fisherman.
Before the mountain
　　the indifferent stream flows on in emptiness,
still going by, as at that time,
　　the jade-treed village.

Zhang Jie (836-905)

桃源

絕壁相欹是洞門，
昔人從此入仙源。
數株花下逢珠翠，
半曲歌中老子孫。
別后自疑園吏夢，
歸來誰信釣翁言。
山前空有無情水，
猶繞當時碧樹村。

章碣

16 Zhuangzi and his butterfly dream

Jin Changxu (fl. late Tang)

Jin Changxu's only surviving poem is "A Spring Complaint" (often translated as "Spring Lament"). It is recognized as a fine example of the five-character quatrain (jueju). Nothing else is known about him.

A Spring Complaint (A Yizhou Song)

Drive off the orioles;
don’t let them sing on the branches.
Their singing shatters my concubine dreams
and I can’t reach Liaoxi.

Jin Changxu (fl. late Tang)

春怨（一作伊州歌）

打起黃鶯兒，
莫教枝上啼。
啼時驚妾夢，
不得到遼西。

金昌緒

Cui Tu (854-?)

Cui was born in what is now Zhejian province. In 888 he passed the imperial examinations (*jinshi*) and held some minor posts. Later, he wandered across China. Not much else is known of him.

Much of his poetry is on the hardships of his journeys. His poems were in the style of the times. He was adept at descriptions of nature and expressing his moods and thoughts. Two of his poems appear in *300 Tang Poems*.

The Solitary Goose

Several flocks have already returned to the frontier;
lone figure, what are you going to do?
In the rain at dusk you call out for them;
it is late when you want to descend to the cold pond.
Banks of low clouds pass in the darkness;
the cold frontier moon follows.
You mustn’t be shot by the stringed arrow;
flying alone, take care!

Cui Tu (854-?)

孤雁

几行歸塞盡，
片影獨何之？
暮雨相呼失，
寒塘欲下遲。
渚雲低暗渡，
關月冷相隨。
未必逢矰繳，
孤飛自可疑。

崔塗

Song Dynasty (960–1279) and later

After the Tang dynasty fell there was a chaotic period of the Five Dynasties and Ten Kingdoms (907–979). But in 960, Emperor Taizu (927–976) of the Song seized power and established the Song dynasty. The Northern Song (960–1127) had its capital at Dongjing (now Kaifeng City). The government structured itself on the Tang legacy and at first it prospered and even expanded its territory. But in 1126, Jurchens invaded from the north and captured Dongjing. Emperor Huizong was captured but one of his sons, proclaimed himself Emperor Gaozong, and fled south, establishing the Southern Song (1127–1279) with its capital at Lin'an (Hangzhou).The Southern Song was prosperous but weak and finally the Mongols, under Kublai Khan, conquered the Song in 1276 and established the Yuan dynasty.

Printing flourished in the Song and literature became accessible to more people. The *ci* form was finally established through the work of Su Shi, who expanded its themes, and it became the dominant form. The early years saw a continuation of Late Tang style but some, such as Lin Bu (967–1028) returned to a simpler approach. Su Shi (1036–1101) is the greatest Song poet but Ouyang Xiu (1007–1072) is not far behind. Other noteworthy poets include Wang Anshi (1021–1086), Huang Tingjian (1045–1105) and Yang Wanli (1127–1206). China's greatest woman poet, Li Qingzhao (1084–1151), belongs to this era as well.

Yuan Dynasty (1271–1368)

The Yuan dynasty was part of the Great Mongol Empire. At first, very strong with able leaders, over time the quality of the rulers declined and the unrest of the populace grew. This lead finally to their overthrow by the Ming in 1368.

In the realm of literature, drama was the main form. Poetry did not flourish other than a *qu*, which were poems included in the plays and related to the *ci*. It was a popular vernacular form. Just like the *ci*, they were set to song patterns, in this case, about three hundred and fifty. The greatest *qu* poet was the playwright Ma Zhiyuan (c. 1260–1334).

Ming Dynasty (1368–1644)

The Ming dynasty was founded by Zhu Yuanzhang in the south. During the Ming there were vast construction projects, including the Forbidden City in Beijing, where the capital was moved to, and the rebuilt Great wall. The army was increased to about one million and there was territorial expansion. Trade, including trade with Europe, grew. Overall there was stability and prosperity. However, in the end, the combination of peasant revolts in the south and Manchu insurgency in the north lead to the demise of the dynasty.

During the Ming, Tang poetry was emulated, leading to a lack of creativity. Although there were innumerable poets, none are regarding as outstanding, although there may be some hidden gems. Some poets regarded Song poetry as the pinnacle and wrote in a more self-expressive manner. Major figures include Gao Qi (1336–1374), Li Dongyang (1447–1516) and Yuan Hongdao

(1568–1610). On the painter-poet side, there are Shen Zhou (1427–1509), Tang Yin (1470–1524) and Wen Zhengming (1470–1559).

Qing Dynasty (1644–1912)

The Qing dynasty reached its peak in the late eighteenth century but foreign interventions, revolts and worsening economic conditions, along with an inflexible bureaucracy, led to a slow decline. The invasion of foreign powers to crush the Boxer Rebellion made the situation untenable and in 1912 the dynasty and imperial rule were abolished and a republican government was established.

During the Qing, the novel was the predominant genre. In poetry, fixation on the past led to a stultification of form. Still, there were some fine poets. Outstanding was Yuan Mei (1716–1797) who valued freedom via creativity and self-expression. He also advocated women's literacy and fostered women poets. His poems express his innermost feelings and are skilfully crafted. Other notable poets are Wu Weiye (1609–1671) and Nalan Xinde (1655–1685) who both excelled in the *ci* form. A fine female poet of the Qing is Wu Zao (1799–1862).

Modern Era (1912-present)

Although the modernist views of Hu Shi (1891–1962) and others led to the demise of classical verse and the rise of Western-influenced themes and forms, some still continued to write in the old manner. Most notable is Mao Zedong (1892–1976). He obviously had a modern sensibility but expressed his, mostly political, thoughts and feelings, in the classical forms.

Lin Bu (967-1028)

Lin Bu was born at Hangzhou. He studied the classics at an early age. He then took to a life of wandering. The last twenty years of his life, he lived as a recluse on Gushan Island on West Lake, near Hangzhou. He never married and referred to the plum blossoms on the many trees he had planted, as his “wife”, and the two tame cranes he kept, as his “children.” Later on this would spawn a whole art tradition, depicting Lin Bu by his plum blossoms and with his cranes. He grew vegetables, gathered fruit and fished for his sustenance. His fame spread and there were many visitors. He was also know as a painter and calligrapher, although only three of the latter survive. Two emperors had sent food to Lin and also requested him to enter public service, which he declined. He studied Buddhism and conversed with monks in nearby temples. After he died he was buried on Gushan and his tomb is now a tourist attraction.

About 330 of his poems survive. Lin Bu was rather the opposite of Bai Juyi in that the latter strove to see that his poems were preserved while Lin was indifferent about the whole matter. He wrote mostly about the scenery and his excursions on West Lake. His poems have a feeling of tranquillity and the style tends to the plain and simple versus the complexities of the Late Tang.

Lin Bu was quite famous in his time. Young literati like Ouyang Xiu (1007–1072) and Mei Yaochen (1002–1060), would come and visit him. In the next generation, the great Su Shi extolled him and composed “Writing a Poem after Lin Bu.” However, he gradually went out of favor. In studies and translations in English, he is quite neglected and there is, for example, no article devoted to him in the *Indiana Companion to Chinese Literature*. For this reason I am including a relatively large number of his poems.

A Recluse's Dwelling on the Lake

Lake water washes up to the fence;
            mountains surround my dwelling.
A recluse's hut should be
            isolated from the world.
The little used door is covered
            with green moss.
When visitors arrive
            the startled white birds fly off.
Sell medicine? You'll just quarrel
            about the price.
I finish watering the garden
            and love the artless way.
What about travelling India Road
            that goes through the forest?
It's like trying to reach the depths of autumn
            in a dream of blue mountain haze.

Lin Bu (967-1028)

湖上隱居

湖水入籬山繞舍，
隱居應與世相違。
閑門自掩蒼苔色，
來客時驚白鳥飛。
賣藥比嘗嫌有價，
灌園終亦愛無機。
如何天竺林間路，
猶到秋深夢翠微。

林逋

A Spring Day on West Lake

My talent can’t compare
with Du Mu’s.
But I’ve come to the lake
to try and write a poem.
Through the spring mist, the dinner drum is struck
in the temple courtyard.
In the twilight are towers, terraces
and tavern banners.
The air is thick with mingled fragrances
from the lower cliffs.
Flying low, two kingfishers
skim the surface of the water.
The human world is fortunate:
one has grass raincoats, bamboo hats,
and can board a boat
and become a fisherman.

Lin Bu (967-1028)

西湖春日

爭得才如杜牧之，
試來湖上輒題詩。
春煙寺院敲齋鼓，
夕照樓台卓酒旗。
濃吐雜芳薰巘崿，
溼飛雙翠破漣漪。
人間幸有蓑兼笠，
且上漁舟作釣師。

林逋

A Winter Evening in a Mountain Village

By the door of my thatched cottage at the foot of the mountain,
spring colors are already appearing.
Bamboos bend under the cold bluish snow;
the evening is scented by plum blossoms falling in the breeze.
It is time to go out on my own and gather firewood;
I'm not at all busy serving tea.
Two egrets sometimes stir
and fly off, straight across field and pond.

Lin Bu (967-1028)

山村冬暮

衡茅林麓下，
春色已微茫。
雪竹低寒翠，
風梅落晚香。
樵期多獨往，
茶事不全忙。
雙鷺有時起，
橫飛過野塘。

林逋

An Evening View from the Lakeside Tower

Lake water drifts along under the blue sky;
leaning on the railing it is tiresome to focus on one thing.
The cold mountains at dusk are wave after wave of emerald green;
in the pureness of autumn, birds are flying high.
Far off thoughts drift more than a thousand miles;
this fleeting life is as light as a single hair.
The trees in the dense forest are innumerable;
a fishing boat fades from view in the thick haze.

Lin Bu (967-1028)

湖樓晚望

湖水混空碧，
憑闌凝睇勞。
夕寒山翠重，
秋淨鳥行高。
遠意極千里，
浮生輕一毫。
叢林數未遍，
杳靄隔漁舠。

林逋

Bamboo Grove

From both sides slant a thousand green tips
over the temple fence.
The mountain path penetrates deeply
through ten thousand flourishing bamboo shoots.
Now I can recall the hall
in your noble house;
when we looked at the painting on the white wall
and counted the stalks.

Lin Bu (967-1028)

竹林

寺籬斜夾千梢翠，
山徑深穿萬籜乾。
卻憶貴家廳館里，
粉牆時畫數莖看。

林逋

Boating on West Lake by Lingyun Temple

Water reflects the light of the sky
    from the slow moving waves.
In the distance are countless blue mountains,
    peak after peak.
Far off, white cranes turn their backs
    to the people this autumn season.
In the evening, a dense grey mist rolls in,
    enveloping the trees.
There's Paulownia Road which runs by
    Seven Mile Rapids,
between Pengli Lake
    and Wulao Peak.
To stop rowing and just drift around till late
    is better than returning home.
Above, from the holy residence,
    the slow tolling of the temple bell.

Lin Bu (967-1028)

西湖泛舟入靈隱寺

水天相映淡溦溶，
隔水青山無數重。
白鳥背人秋自遠，
蒼煙和樹晚來濃。
桐廬道次七里瀨，
彭蠡湖間五老峰。
輟棹遲回比未得，
上方精舍動疏鐘。

林逋

By Chance Out on the Lake in Early Spring

The plum trees' bloom has come and gone,
and year-end has likewise passed.
The spring is warm as always
and it's Cold Food Festival time.
Their vital colors have half-returned
to the willows by the shore.
Crowds of people board boats
by the town gates.
Bright-colored birds, side-by-side,
are resplendent on the short grass.
A fine mist is about to float up
over the green waves.
In several places wine shop banners
shadowed by mountains,
flutter in the breeze, sounding
like stringed instruments.

Lin Bu (967-1028)

湖上初春偶作

梅花開盡臘亦盡，
春暖便如寒食天。
氣色半歸湖岸柳，
人家多上郭門船。
文禽相并映短草，
翠瀲欲生浮嫩煙。
几處酒旗山影下，
細風時已弄繁弦。

林逋

Chiyang Mountain Inn

Many village homes and shops
are clustered by the mountain.
It is already sunset when I dismount from my horse
by the dilapidated bridge.
Startled birds suddenly fly quickly away,
disturbing the mist over a mountain stream.
Hidden flowers flutter down in the breeze
into the moat, perfuming the air.
While I am moored here
my heart yet rejoices;
In days after, trying to think about these times
will drive me mad.
I regret turning around
at the single shrill note of a flute.
The tavern banners slant up fluttering
on thin bamboo poles.

Lin Bu (967-1028)

池陽山店

數家村店簇山旁，
下馬危橋已夕陽。
驚鳥忽沖篠靄破，
暗花閑墮塹風香。
時間槃泊心猶戀，
日后尋思興必狂。
可惜回頭一聲笛，
酒旗斜曳出疏篁。

林逋

Frosty Weather at the Break of Dawn

Pure ice, crystal frost; it looks like
plum blossoms bloomed last night.
Where did the three jade dragons[17] frolic,
their roars causing tremor upon tremor?
I dreamed of a pure golden beast,
but by cold dawn the dream's fragrant embers had vanished.
I want to roll back the curtains to enjoy this vision of purity:
no one has swept the snow from the front steps yet!

Lin Bu (967-1028)

霜天曉角

冰清霜潔，
昨夜梅花發。
甚處玉龍三弄，
聲搖動，聲搖動？
夢金獸絕，
曉寒蘭燼滅。
要卷珠簾清賞，
且莫掃，階前雪！

林逋

17 Associated with the weather, especially storms.

Huangjia Village

My boat's tied up
by the banks of Huangjia Village.
This stream is always fine
to moor here for the night.
The countryside inspires me
to seek out many bamboo trails.
Local customs impel me
to visit a few teahouses.
A frightened calf bleats, in the rain and dark,
near a remote village.
Gulls descend in the evening
to the low flat shoreline.
Then there's the brocade boats
where people indulge in licentiousness.
Poetic sorrow follows
when there are no limits.

Lin Bu (967-1028)

黃家莊

黃家莊畔一維舟，
總是沿流好宿頭。
野興几多尋竹徑，
風情些小上茶樓。
遙村雨暗鳴寒犢，
淺漵沙平下晚鷗。
更有錦帆荒蕩事，
茫茫隨分起詩愁。

林逋

Kitten

From time to time it delicately snags
fish from the creek.
Sated, lying in the flowery shade,
it is doing exceedingly well.
Naturally, rats despise me –
as I'm poor, they never come.
And I'm not ashamed to have
an idler living in my hut.

Lin Bu (967-1028)

貓兒

纎鈎時得小溪魚，
飽臥花陰興有余。
自是鼠嫌貧不到，
莫慚尸素在吾廬。

林逋

Leisurely Boating on West Lake on an Autumn's Day

Mist over the water merges with the shadowed mountains;
in this vastness, it's already autumn.
I enjoy the view of a temple deep in the forest;
I regret leaving the tranquil banks as the boat glides by.
Thin reeds bend in the first cold;
a partial rainbow arcs at the fall of dusk.
Whereabouts is my cottage?
Time to go back; I'll chant a fisherman's song on the way.

Lin Bu (967-1028)

秋日西湖閒泛

水氣并山影，
蒼茫已作秋。
林深喜見寺，
岸靜惜移舟。
疏葦先寒折，
殘虹帶夕收。
吾廬在何處，
歸興起漁謳。

林逋

Ouyang Xiu (1007– 1072)

Ouyang Xiu was raised in what is now Hubei after the early death of his father. In his studies, he came across the writings of the neglected Han Yu and was influenced both by his plain prose style and his Confucianism. He later became an acclaimed prose master in the Han Yu style. He passed the imperial examinations (*jinshi*) in 1030 and embarked on a successful career as an official in Luoyang. He retired in 1071 and died the following year. He was heavily involved in politics and also wrote works on history, notably *The New History of the Tang*, He also wrote a work on poetics, *Mr. One-six's Talks on Poetics*. He was the first great literati of the Song dynasty.

Ouyang wrote *shu* and *ci*. His old-style poems, especially in his later years show a preference for the plain and simple versus Late Tang ornateness and complexity. He also used odd line lengths to provide variety. These poems show a lightness and serenity. He also introduced new themes before considered mundane. His *ci* were often on erotic subjects. There were widely appreciated and further spread the popularity of the form. Ouyang was a great influence on is contemporaries. However, as outstanding as Ouyang Xiu was, he was soon to be overshadowed by Su Shi.

Picking Mulberries

The fresh, lovely flowers are past,
but West Lake is fine –
damaged remnants of red scattered about
and flying catkins like mist.
The weeping willow's trunk
is worn by sun and wind.

Reed pipes and singing gradually cease
as visitors leave,
and I become aware of the spring sky.
I pull down the window's curtains
as a pair of swallows come winging home
through a light drizzle.

Ouyang Xiu (1007– 1072)

采桑子・群芳過后西湖好

群芳過后西湖好，
狼籍殘紅，
飛絮濛濛。
垂柳闌干盡日風。

笙歌散盡游人去，
始覺春空。
垂下簾櫳，
雙燕歸來細雨中。

歐陽修

Wang Anshi (1021-1086)

Wang Anshi was born in Jiangxi and passed the imperial examinations (*jinshi*) in 1042. Rising through the official ranks, he was appointed vice-counsellor in 1069 and implemented his "New Policies", an overall reform of administrative policies. Many were opposed (notably Su Shi in the literary realm) and after a famine in north China, he was forced to resign. Reinstated a year later, the environment was no longer conducive to his work and he resigned again shortly thereafter, retiring to Jiangning. His reforms were totally overturned the year before he died.

His surviving poems number more than 1,500. He was a prose master in the Ouyang tradition and in fact, was a protégé of the latter. He wrote mainly old-style verse. His early poems often had a political or social slant. However, his poems written in retirement in four- or eight-stanzas, are his best. There is some Buddhist influence in his work as well. His later works show an effortless simplicity in presentation.

New Year's Day

Amidst the burst of firecrackers,
the old year ends.
The warm spring breeze carries
the scent of Tusu wine[18].
On a thousand gates, ten thousand homes,
the sun beams.
Everywhere, new peach charms
replace the old.

Wang Anshi (1021-1086)

元日

爆竹聲中一歲除，
春風送暖入屠蘇。
千門萬戶瞳瞳日，
總把新桃換舊符。

王安石

18 A traditional Chinese drink at New Year's.

A Journey to Zhong Mountain

The twin peaks' pines and oaks
conceal vermilion vines;
The river here is an easy match
for Wuling's blossoms[19].
From mid-day chanting from behind the clouds,
I know a temple is there.
At sunset, I return home,
not having met one monk.

Wang Anshi (1021–1086)

遊鍾山

兩山松櫟暗朱藤，
一水中間勝武陵。
午梵隔雲知有寺，
夕陽歸去不逢僧。

王安石

19 The fisherman who discovered Peach Blossom Spring in Tao Yuanming's work of that name, was from Wuling, which name became associated with the idyllic paradise.

Su Shi (1037 – 1101)

Su Shi, also known as Su Dongpo, was born in Sichuan to an eminent family. Indeed, along with his father and brother, he was considered one of the finest prose masters of the Tang and Song dynasties. Su Shi took the imperial exam (*jinshi*) in 1057 and was taken under the aegis of Ouyang Xiu, who became his patron. He had a long political struggle against the reformer, Wang Anshi, and was banished many times, the last being to remote Hainan. He died on his recall from there to the capital. Su Shi excelled at poetry (shu, ci fu), prose, painting and calligraphy, as well as being actively involved in politics.

About 2,400 of Su Shi's poems survive along with 350 *ci*. The latter, he expanded to cover more serious themes and changed the nature of the genre. He was influenced by Tao Yuanming and wrote a number of "imitations" of his poems. He also admired Wang Wei, famously referring to the poetry of his paintings and the painting elements of his poetry. Su had Daoist and Buddhist leanings and a yearning for reclusion, although he was too political to ever follow that through. In addition to poems with a philosophical tinge, he wrote on the pleasures and pains of everyday life. There was an exuberance in his work that can perhaps be traced to his Sichuan upbringing (note also Li Bai in this regard). Overall, Su Shi is an outstanding figure of Chinese literature.

Mid-Autumn Moon

At twilight, the gathered clouds disperse in the distance;
it is clear and cold.
The Silver River silently floats over
the jade dish[20].
This life, this night,
will not be this good for long –
next year, where I will be,
gazing at the bright moon?

Su Shi (1037 – 1101)

中秋月

暮雲收盡溢清寒，
銀漢無聲轉玉盤。
此生此夜不長好，
明月明年何處看。

蘇軾

20 Silver River and jade dish – Milky Way and the moon respectively.

Yang Wanli (1127–1206)

Yang was born in Jiangxi. He passed the imperial examinations (*jinshi*) in 1154. He then served in various posts. He was governor of Guangdong in about 1180 and put down a rebellion there. As a reward he was recalled to the capital but afterwards clashed with the emperor and was given provincial posts again. He resigned from one post in 1192 in protest against Song dynasty monetary polices. On his death he was survived by his wife, who appears to have been a remarkable woman, three sons and a daughter.

Yang Wanli was included in the Four Masters of Southern Song Poetry. He imitated the five-character regulated verse of Chen Shitao and the seven-character verse of Wang Anshi and the late Tang writers. In 1178 he had a poetic epiphany that caused him to burn most of his poems (over a thousand) and start anew. He developed a Chan Buddhist based poetics that stressed spontaneity and naturalness that was to impact later theorists. He wrote on a wide variety of subjects but nature, including landscape, plants and animals, looms large. He also wrote realistically about peasant life. Lastly, he expresses an alienation from society due to his transcendent ideals. In all over 4,200 of his poems survive, which is indeed a huge number.

South Creek at Sunset

The creek reflects the blazing twilight
as the month comes to an end,
and water babbles against the rocks
amidst the fine sand.
I want to return to my childhood,
and dwell by the young fish,
watching leaping waves
form into jade rings.

Yang Wanli (1127–1206)

南溪暮立

溪影明霞新月底
水声乱石嫩沙间。
欲归小为鱼儿住
更看跳波玉一环。

楊萬里

The Small Pond

At the fount’s opening,
the cherished delicate flow.
Shaded trees reflect off the water,
delighted with the clear gentleness.
The young lotus have just revealed
their pointed shoots,
but right away, dragonflies
perch on their tips.

Yang Wanli (1127–1206)

小池

泉眼無聲惜細流
樹陰照水愛晴柔。
小荷才露尖尖角
早有蜻蜓立上頭。

楊萬里

Yuan Mei (1716–1797)

Yuan Mei was born in Hangzhou to a cultured family. He passed the imperial examinations (*jinshi*) in 1739. He assumed various posts but in 1748, he resigned to focus on his literary pursuits. He had a special interest in the education of women, admired much poetry by women and as well, directed a school of women poets. Two of his sisters were well-known poets. He travelled extensively in south China and besides poetry, wrote ghost stories.

Yuan's poetry was written in a direct and simple language and was often what we might term, confessional. His poems are numerous and on a variety of topics. Influenced by Chan Buddhism he wrote literary essays, most notably *Poetry Talks from Sui Garden*. He rejected imitation of past masters and advocated expressing one's own feelings while still keeping a focus on poetic technique.

A Chance Encounter

By chance, passing over a blue creek,
haze floating over fields and water,
a fishing pole was on the ground,
but I saw no one fishing.

Yuan Mei (1716–1797)

偶過

偶過青溪上，
濛濛野水春。
釣魚竿在地，
不見釣魚人。

袁枚

A Visitor

In the evening I sought out a visitor to the mountains;
the moon was glowing through the haze.
I knocked at the gate, but no one seemed to be there –
just the crane of the Immortals uttered a single cry.

Yuan Mei (1716–1797)

訪客

夜訪山中客，
濛濛月色凝。
敲門人未覺，
仙鶴一聲應。

袁枚

Mao Zedong (1893–1976)

Mao Zedong was born in Henan to a well-off peasant family. He early on, got caught up with the Chinese Communist Party (he was a founding member) and spent years in various conflicts culminating in the Communist victory in 1949. He was made Chairman and remained so until the end of his life.

Mao wrote about forty poems in classical forms. His poems express his aspirations and show some technical innovation. He felt though, that China in the modern age should look at new literary forms and as such, he is in a sense, at the terminus of Chinese poetry in classical forms. All his poetry was essentially political, but "Yellow Crane Tower" can be read on its own terms.

Yellow Crane Tower

Vast, vast the nine tributaries[21] flow through our land;
deep, deep one route passing from south to north.
Through the misty rain, the lush vegetation is gray;
Tortoise and Snake lock up the great river[22].
The yellow crane has gone, who knows where?
What remains is a site for visitors.
My wine, I sprinkle in libation to the surging waters –
my heart wells up with each swelling wave.

Mao Zedong (1893–1976)

黄鶴樓

茫茫九派流中國，
沉沉一線穿南北。
煙雨莽蒼蒼，
龜蛇鎖大江。
黄鶴知何去？
剩有游人處。
把酒酹滔滔，
心潮逐浪高！

毛澤東

21 Of the Yangtze.
22 The great river is the Yangtze which is flanked by Tortoise and Snake hills.

Selected Bibliography

Barnsone, Tony, and Chou Ping. *The Anchor Book of CHINESE POETRY.* New York: Anchor Books, 2004.

Chang, Kang-i Sun. *Six Dynasties Poetry*. Princeton: Princeton University Press, 1986.

Davis, A. R. *T'ao Yuan-ming: His Works and Their Meaning,* 2 vols. Cambridge: Cambridge University Press, 1983.

Fuller, James R. *The Road to East Slope: The Development of Su Shi's Poetic Voice*. Standford: Stanford University Press, 1990.

Hawkes, David. *The Songs of the South: An Ancient Chinese Anthology of Poems by Qu Yuan and Other Poets.* London: Penguin Books, 1985.

Karlgren, Bernhard. *The Book of Odes: Chinese Text, Transcription and Translation*. Stockholm: The Museum of Far Eastern Antiquities, 1974.

Liu, James J. Y. *Major Lyricists of the Northern Sung: A.D 960-1126.* Princeton: Princeton University Press, 1974.

________. *The Art of Chinese Poetry.* Chicago: The University of Chicago Press, 1962.

Liu, Wu-chi, and Irving Yucheng Lo. *The Sunflower Splendor: Three Thousand Years of Chinese Poetry*. New York: Anchor Press, 1975.

Nienhauser, William H. *The Indiana companion to traditional Chinese Literature*. 2 Vols. Bloomington: Indiana University Press, 1998.

Owen, Stephen. *The Great Age of Chinese Poetry: The High T'ang*. New Haven: The Yale University Press, 1981.

________. *The Late Tang: Chinese Poetry of the Mid-Ninth Century.* Harvard East Asian Monographs No. 264. Cambridge: Harvard University Asia Center, 2006.

________. *The Making of Early Classical Chinese Poetry.* Harvard East Asian Monographs No. 261. Cambridge: Harvard University Asia Center, 2006.

Rouzer, Paul. *The Poetry and Prose of Wang Wei.* 2 vols. Boston/Berlin: de Gruyter, 2020.

Seaton, J. P. *Bright Moon, White Clouds: Selected Poems of Li Po.* Boston: Shambhala Publications, 2012.

Trotter, Earl. *Tao Yuanming: The Complete Works.* Chatham: Peach Blossom Press, 2020.

Watson, Burton. *Su T'ung-Po: Selections from a Sung Dynasty Poet.* New York & London: Columbia University Press, 1965.

Yoshikawa, Kojiro. *An Introduction to Sung Poetry* (Burton Watson trans.). Harvard Yenching Institute Monograph Volume XVII. Cambridge: Harvard University Press, 1967.

www.ingramcontent.com/pod-product-compliance
Ingram Content Group UK Ltd.
Pitfield, Milton Keynes, MK11 3LW, UK
UKHW020142250726
13967UKWH00002B/811